Masters: Art Quilts

JANE SASSAMAN ■ MICHAEL A. CUMMINGS ■
ITA ZIV ■ CHER CARTWRIGHT ■ NORIKO ENDO
■ DEIDRE SCHERER ■ CAROLYN L. MAZLOOMI ■
HOLLIS CHATELAIN ■ LINDA COLSH ■ CHARLOTTE YDE
■ JOAN SCHULZE ■ JUDITH CONTENT ■
KYOUNG AE CHO ■ JETTE CLOVER
■ ESZTER BORNEMISZA ■ PAULINE BURBIDGE ■
YVONNE PORCELLA ■ M. JOAN LINTAULT
■ KATIE PASQUINI MASOPUST ■ NANCY N. ERICKSON ■

■ SUSAN SHIE ■ CARYL BRYER FALLERT ■
JEANETTE GILKS ■ JANE BURCH COCHRAN
■ PAMELA ALLEN ■ THERESE MAY ■ JOHN W. LEFELHOCZ ■
MIRIAM NATHAN-ROBERTS ■ JENNY HEARN
■ TERRIE HANCOCK MANGAT ■ WENDY HUHN ■ B.J. ADAMS ■
INGE MARDAL & STEEN HOUGS ■ CHIAKI DOSHO
■ INGE HUEBER ■ MICHAEL JAMES ■ VELDA E. NEWMAN ■
ANNE WORINGER ■ CLARE PLUG
■ ELIZABETH BRIMELOW

Masters: Art Quilts

Major Works by Leading Artists

Martha Sielman, author and curator

LARK BOOKS
A Division of Sterling Publishing Co., Inc.
New York / London

DEVELOPMENT EDITORS

Ray Hemachandra

James Knight

EDITOR

Nathalie Mornu

ART DIRECTOR

Kathleen Holmes

COVER DESIGNER

Cindy LaBreacht

COVER, LEFT TO RIGHT

Cher Cartwright
Recurrent, 2003
Photo by Ken Mayer

Ita Ziv
Inner Struggle, 2006
Photo by Ran Erde

Pamela Allen
*Lillian Hellman Taking the Oath Before
HUAC,* 2002
Photo by artist

Caryl Bryer Fallert
Spirogyra, 2002
Photo by artist

Jane Sassaman
Overgrown Garden, 1994
Photo by Gregory Gantner

BACK COVER, LEFT TO RIGHT

Susan Shie
Year of the Dog, 2006
Photo by artist

Chiaki Dosho
Cherry Blossom, 2005
Photo by T. Kobe

Therese May
I Am Who I Am, 2003

Library of Congress Cataloging-in-Publication Data

Sielman, Martha.
  Masters : art quilts / Martha Sielman. -- 1st ed.
      p. cm.
  Includes index.
  ISBN-13: 978-1-60059-107-5 (PB-trade pbk. : alk. paper)
  ISBN-10: 1-60059-107-8 (PB-trade pbk. : alk. paper)
 1. Art quilts--United States--History--20th century. 2. Art
quilts--United States--History--21st century. I. Title.
  NK9112.S52 2008
  746.460973--dc22

                                          2007031080

10 9 8 7 6 5 4 3 2 1

First Edition

Published by Lark Books, A Division of
Sterling Publishing Co., Inc.
387 Park Avenue South, New York, NY 10016

Text © 2008, Lark Books
Photography © 2008, Artist/Photographer as specified

Distributed in Canada by Sterling Publishing,
c/o Canadian Manda Group, 165 Dufferin Street
Toronto, Ontario, Canada M6K 3H6

Distributed in the United Kingdom by GMC Distribution Services,
Castle Place, 166 High Street, Lewes, East Sussex, England BN7 1XU

Distributed in Australia by Capricorn Link (Australia) Pty Ltd.,
P.O. Box 704, Windsor, NSW 2756 Australia

If you have questions or comments about this book, please contact:
Lark Books
67 Broadway
Asheville, NC 28801
(828) 253-0467

Manufactured in China

ISBN 13: 978-1-60059-107-5
ISBN 10: 1-60059-107-8

For information about custom editions, special sales, and premium and corporate purchases, please
contact the Sterling Special Sales Department at 800-805-5489 or specialsales@sterlingpub.com.

Contents

Introduction

When people ask me how I got involved with art quilts, I tell them it all began when I was very little and my mother let me play with the fabric scraps left over from sewing our dresses. Whenever I talk about playing with those fabrics, my hands automatically start to mime touching the pieces—feeling the bumpiness of corduroy, the softness of velveteen, the slinky smoothness of sateen, and the crinkly quality of seersucker.

I made my first quilt in 1988. I saw an alphabet quilt in a magazine and wanted to make one for my baby. I went to the Hartford Public Library in Connecticut and borrowed every book it had on quilting—all six of them. I went to my local dress-fabric store (I knew of no quilting stores) and bought the only material it had for quilting: pastel calico cottons.

But I was hooked. I eventually found Roberta Horton's book *The Fabric Makes the Quilt*, which encouraged my experimentation. I made a quilt based on my own design in 1995 and haven't looked back. Today, of course, books about quilting line shelf after bookstore shelf—and you can't find a store devoted to dress fabrics anymore—but my history is fairly typical of the experience of many art quilters.

The art-quilt movement in the United States began at the Whitney Museum of American Art in New York City. The Whitney's 1971 exhibit Abstract Design in American Quilts moved the Amish quilt collection of Jonathan Holstein and Gail van der Hoof off the bed and onto museum walls, showing quilts to be artworks with strong visual connections to contemporary painting. The United States' bicentennial in 1976 revived American interest in traditional quilt making, and the feminist movement championed raising the status of "women's work," such as quilting. But it took a long time for quilting, and in particular art quilting, to become established in the art world.

Milestones were reached, one after another. The first Quilt National exhibit, a biennial, international juried competition celebrating the quilt as an art form, took place in 1979. Penny McMorris' public-television series interviewing contemporary quilters aired in 1981. The term "art quilt" was coined in 1984 as the title of the traveling exhibit The Art Quilt, organized by McMorris and Michael Kile. The Women of Color Quilters Network was founded by Carolyn L. Mazloomi in 1985, and Studio Art Quilt Associates, or SAQA, a nonprofit resource and advocacy membership organization, was founded by Yvonne Porcella in 1989.

As the art movement grew in the United States, art-quilt movements began in other countries. Some artists report being directly influenced by exhibits or publications of American art quilts, while others developed independently and only discovered what was happening in America after art quilting had been established in their homelands. Art quilting has benefited from globalization, as organizations and publications have become increasingly international. Artists travel all over the world to teach fellow enthusiasts.

I have been honored to curate this book of master art quilters—artists recognized over the years for the excellence of their work and whose art has been influential in the development of the field. But the job has not been easy. When the editors at Lark Books asked Caryl Bryer Fallert for advice on developing this project, she sat down and immediately came up with a list of 200 art quilters who warranted inclusion. Many wonderful artists have been critical in the development of this art form, but only 40 people are included in each volume of the *Masters* series. I hope this sampling of leading artists delights and inspires you, and moves you to explore further the wonderful art-quilt work showcased in exhibits and catalogs and on websites such as www.saqa.com.

The book's underlying concept of displaying up to a dozen quilts by each of the artists does limit the number of quilters included in the book, but it also allows the artists' work to be seen in much greater depth. The result is an incredibly rich visual feast which provides an opportunity to learn more about each artist than would be possible in a survey of only one or two seminal works per quilter.

In viewing the quilts and reading the artists' ruminations about their work, you will gain an understanding of the pathways the quilters have taken, the themes they explore, and the questions they return to time and again. The artists have diverse aspirations, approaches, and techniques, so you will find enormous variation—and beauty in many guises—in these quilts.

In curating the book, I feel like I have been a privileged guest invited to enter the artists' worlds to gain a deeper understanding of their art. I am very pleased to extend that invitation to you in the pages that follow.

Martha Sielman
Executive Director
Studio Art Quilt Associates

Jane Sassaman

JAM-PACKED WITH DRAMA is how Jane Sassaman describes gardens, which inspire her work. The flowers, she says, display attitude and theatrical spectacle. In translating them into formally symmetrical designs reminiscent of William Morris, Sassaman focuses as much on the thorns as on the roses and joins them together in a stylized ballet. Often outlined dramatically in black, her meticulously appliquéd forms curl and coil around one another. While she has made numerous pieces celebrating the tree of life, Sassaman has created almost as many pieces focusing on nature's cycles of destruction and decay. A repeating element in many of her works is the spiky seedpod of the jimsonweed plant (also called angel's trumpet or thorn apple), which she describes as having "wonderfully evil-looking spiky seed balls the size of Christmas tree ornaments." In the past few years, insects have made an appearance in her work, becoming a part of Sassaman's continuing exploration of the garden's natural cycles.

▲ Willow | 1996

75 x 75 inches (1.9 x 1.9 m)
Machine appliquéd and quilted
Photos by Gregory Gantner

▲ **Trouble in the Garden** | 1993

61 x 77 inches (1.6 x 2 m)
Machine appliquéd and quilted

Photo by Gregory Gantner

" Most of my quilts are symbolic statements about the cycles and spiritual forces of life. Plants are my metaphor. A plant travels the same cycle as a human: fertility, birth, maturity, death, and rebirth. "

▲ **Iris 2** | 2000
30 x 30 inches (76.2 x 76.2 cm)
Cottons; machine appliquéd
Photos by Gregory Gantner

◄ **Metamorphosis** | 2000
78 x 29 inches (198.1 x 73.7 cm)
Cottons; machine appliquéd
Photos by Brian Blauser

▲ **Heaven's Gift** | 1990

  60 x 78 inches (1.5 x 2 m)
  Machine appliquéd and quilted
  Photo by Judy Smith-Kressley

" Every day I give thanks that I am able to do what I love. Quilt making provides all the elements that satisfy my soul: color, fabric, bold designs, craftsmanship, problem solving, and a challenge for my physical skills. "

▲ Seeds and Blossoms | 1998

43 x 43 inches (1.1 x 1.1 m)
Cottons, textile paint; machine appliquéd, stenciled
Photo by Gregory Gantner

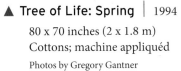

▲ **Tree of Life: Spring** │ 1994

80 x 70 inches (2 x 1.8 m)

Cottons; machine appliquéd

Photos by Gregory Gantner

" I design in a collage technique. I make shapes and weegee them (my name for moving things around, taken from old Ouija boards) until they find their proper places. I enjoy the spontaneity of working this way and feeling the conversation between the shapes. "

◀ **Garden of Shadows** │ 2004
90 x 60 inches (2.3 x 1.5 m)
Cottons, damask; machine appliquéd
Photo by Gregory Gantner

Sprouts | 2000 ▶

24 x 18 inches (61 x 45.7 cm)

Cottons, sheers; machine appliquéd

Photo by Gregory Gantner

▲ **Vortex** | 2000

45 x 41½ inches (1.1 x 1 m)
Cottons; machine appliquéd

Photo by Gregory Gantner

Overgrown Garden | 1994 ▶

41 x 27½ inches (104.1 x 69.9 cm)
Cottons; machine appliquéd
Photos by Gregory Gantner

▲ **Glorious Greens** │ 1998

  61 x 58 inches (1.6 x 1.5 m)
  Cottons; machine appliquéd

  Photos by Gregory Gantner

Michael A. Cummings

THE ENERGY OF MICHAEL A. CUMMINGS' CENTRAL APPLIQUÉD IMAGES threatens to escape the boundaries set by his traditional pieced borders. Combining elements from his African American heritage, Yoruba mythology, and formal art training, his narratives focus on subjects such as jazz musicians, historical heroes, and the Yoruba water goddess. Helper animals and spirit symbols occupy corners or edges of his works, sometimes crawling into the center in their eagerness to be a part of the story. Masks offer layers of meaning that echo the layers of fabric, while glowing yellow accents appear in almost every work, sometimes symbolizing the rhythms of jazz, sometimes the light of heaven. Visual tension is created through the contrast of the orderliness of traditional chintz fabrics and pieced elements with the organized chaos of his appliquéd forms. In trying to create a new aesthetic, Cummings has produced a body of work filled with energy, edginess, and excitement.

African Jazz #5 | 1990 ▶

108 x 72 inches (2.7 x 1.8 m)
Cotton, blends, buttons, textile
paint; appliquéd, machine sewn

Photos by Karen Bell

Christt Bearing Cross | 2003 ▶

72 x 60 inches (1.8 x 1.5 m)
Fabric, African cotton print, satin,
beads; appliquéd, machine and
hand sewn

Photos by Karen Bell

" My African-American quilting heritage is rich in traditions and characterized by storytelling and improvisational styles that were introduced by slaves. In selecting my themes, some may come from personal experiences. I've been influenced by the work of Romare Bearden, cubism, tapestries from Senegal, music, folk arts, and many art forms from around the world. "

◀ Take My Brother Home | 1993

72 x 60 inches (1.8 x 1.5 m)
Cotton, blends, satin, African beadwork, velvet; appliquéd, machine sewn

Photos by Karen Bell

MICHAEL A. CUMMINGS

Absolut Vodka Quilt | 1997 ▶

60 x 48 inches (1.5 x 1.2 m)
Cotton, printed mud cloth, buttons;
appliquéd, machine sewn

Photos by Karen Bell

▲ I'll Fly Away | 1991

90 x 82 inches (2.3 x 2.1 m)
Cottons, blends, African fabric,
fabric, antique quilt blocks

Photos by Karen Bell

▲ **Haitian Mermaid #3** | 1995

  60 x 60 inches (1.5 x 1.5 m)
  Cotton, blends, fabric, velvet, rayon;
  machine sewn, appliquéd
  Photo by Karen Bell

" I have crossed art boundaries, combining quilt techniques and studio art skills—an effect that is conveyed in my construction methods and motifs. Since I started working with quilts, my style has evolved from early experimentation with pieced quilting to my current appliquéd narrative pieces. "

◄ African Jazz #10 | 1990
108 x 72 inches (2.7 x 1.8 m)
Cotton, blends; appliquéd, machine sewn
Photo by Sara Wells

MICHAEL A. CUMMINGS

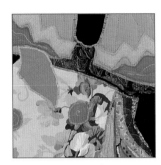

Purplish Cooper | 2001 ▶

72 x 72 inches (1.8 x 1.8 m)
Cotton, linen, blends, silk;
machine sewn

Photos by Karen Bell

◀ **Red Admiral** | 2001

72 x 72 inches (1.8 x 1.8 m)
Cotton, linen, silk; machine
sewn, appliquéd

Photos by Karen Bell

" My quilt themes bring together the art, philosophies, and mythologies of Africans, Europeans, and Americans. I have attempted to create a new aesthetic within the quilt art form. I negotiate a composition's emotional elements by balancing a studio approach with quilting techniques. "

▲ **Storyteller** | 1997

72 x 60 inches (1.8 x 1.5 m)
Textile paint, cotton, African beadwork,
African prints, fabric

Photos by Karen Bell

Ita Ziv

A CELEBRATION OF LIFE is what you sense when viewing the work of Ita Ziv. Playfulness in her use of color and materials is created through dyeing and manipulating a variety of both common and unusual materials, such as plastic and nylon. Ziv makes these materials her own through a series of different processes, which she describes as being akin to a metamorphosis. Brilliantly colored, abstract, appliquéd shapes cascade across the surface of each piece. Her work is inspired by both the natural world and the political conditions around her. (Ziv was born in Poland but moved to Israel at the age of three.) Though primarily composed of simple shapes and lines, Ziv's designs are animated through her use of colors: high-energy reds, oranges, and yellow-greens. Dynamic, invigorating, off-kilter placement moves the viewer's eye around and around the piece until he or she feels Ziv's own joy in her creation. Ziv says, "You are the artist—you have to design your experience with your own hands."

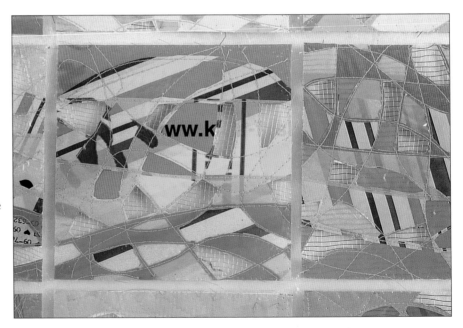

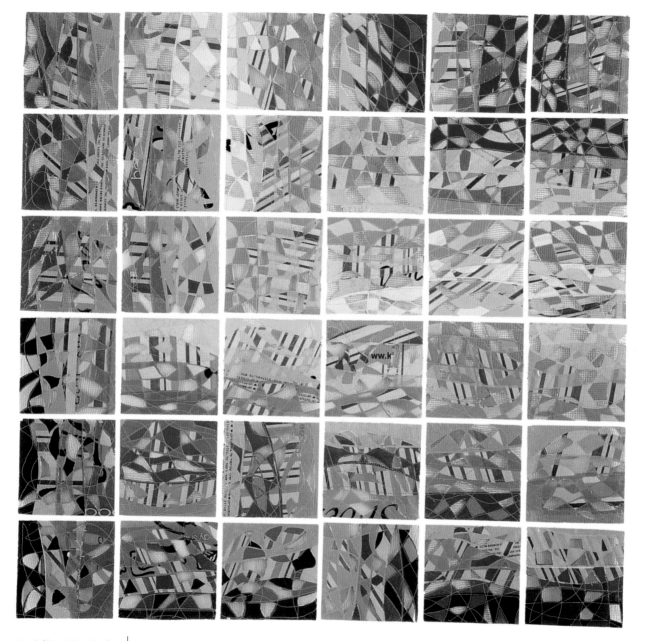

▲ **After the Rain** | 2004

   35½ x 35½ inches (90.2 x 90.2 cm)
   Nylon bags, nets; machine pieced, reverse appliquéd
   Photos by Ran Erde

" When I worked on my first pieces, I found that what I enjoyed most was to treat fabric in unusual ways and change it completely. While undergoing several treatments, the fabric changes in my hands, and it no longer looks the same nor feels the same. "

Explosion | 2002 ▶

47 x 32 inches
(119.4 x 81.3 cm)
Organza, golden metallic
thread; hand dyed,
printed, stamped

Photos by Ran Erde

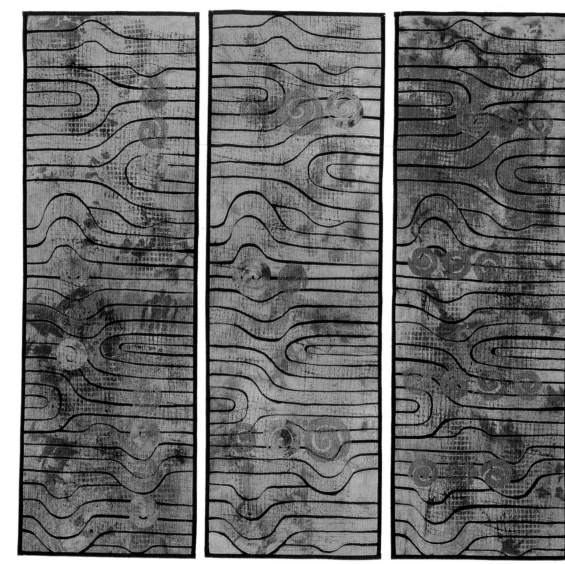

▲ Inner Struggle | 2006

36 x 48 inches (91.4 x 121.9 cm)
Cotton, metallic thread; hand
dyed, fused, free-motion
machine embroidered

Photos by Ran Erde

▲ **Fatem Morgana** | 2007

36 x 49 inches (91.4 x 124.5 cm)
Nylon organza, metallic thread,
gold leaf; hand dyed, shrunk,
collaged, quilted, embroidered

Photos by Ran Erde

" Sometimes, even after treating fabric several times, I feel the need to give it another touch. I fold it or shrink it, print it or stamp it, making even more changes. I sometimes make use of nontraditional materials, such as plastics, nylon bags, transparencies, and netting, using them as if they were textiles. "

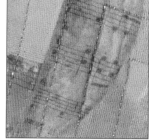

▲ **Musical Partita-Allegro** | 2006

41½ x 35 inches (105.4 x 88.9 cm)
Nylon organza, nylon, metallic threads; hand dyed, printed, machine pieced, fused, free-motion machine embroidered
Photos by Ran Erde

Reflection | 2007 ▶

54 x 19 inches (137.2 x 48.3 cm)
Organza, cotton, metallic thread;
hand dyed, folded, machine
pieced and quilted

Photos by Ran Erde

◀ **Recycling** | 2004

77½ x 23½ inches (196.9 x 59.7 cm)
Nylon bags, golden threads; machine
pieced, reverse appliquéd

Photos by Ran Erde

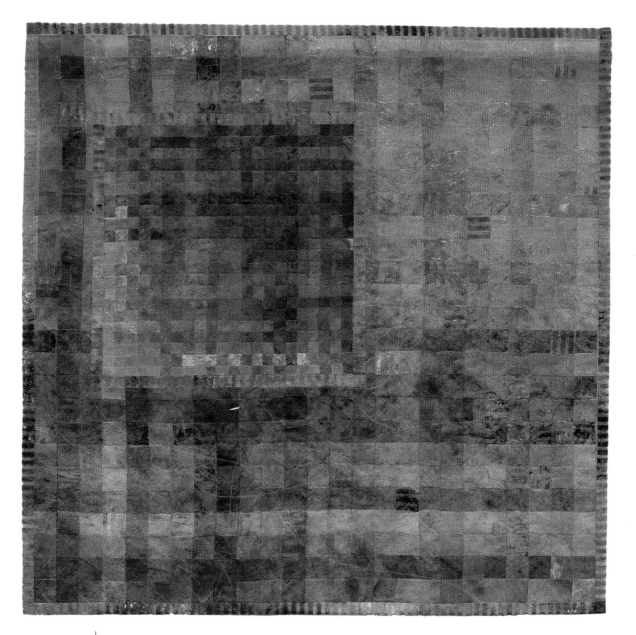

▲ Rainbow | 2004

51 x 51 inches (1.3 x 1.3 m)
Nylon organza, acrylic, metallic thread; hand dyed,
woven, machine quilted and embroidered

Photo by artist

▲ **It's Not Green Anymore, Fire 1** | 2006

47½ x 43½ inches (1.2 x 1.1 m)
Cotton fabrics, rayon thread; hand dyed, fused, machine quilted

Photos by Ran Erde

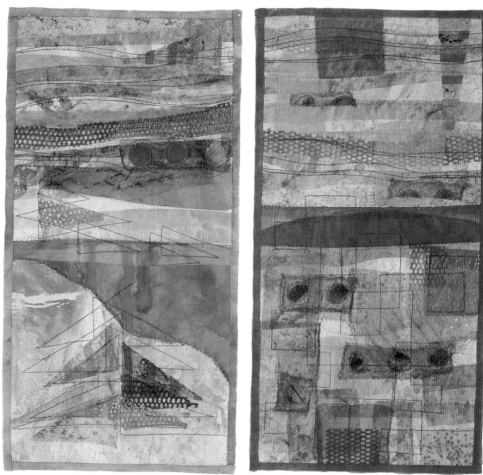

▲ Landscapes | 2005

16 x 25½ inches (40.6 x 64.8 cm)
Nylon organza, metallic threads;
collaged, quilted, embroidered

Photo by Ran Erde

" My quilts deal with my experiences in everyday life. I use them
to express the joy I find in nature, as well as my frustrations
with political situations. Happy occasions, little joys, fresh
flowers after the rain, the wonder of nature's powers—all find
their way into my quilts. "

Cher Cartwright

SOMETIMES ART CAN TRANSFORM YOUR LIFE: Cher Cartwright's life altered dramatically when she went from living what she describes as a monochromatic life as a lawyer to becoming a quilt artist. The Canadian artist discovered the excitement of working with color. Cartwright says she had been oblivious to much of the visual world, so "I was completely surprised at what exploded out of me." Cartwright only uses fabrics she has dyed herself, because she finds the creation of color on cloth to be integral to the joy she finds in making fiber art. Perhaps also in contrast to the linear thinking of her former profession, she concentrated for many years on curves and circles, fascinated by the play of color and fluidity she could achieve using improvisationally pieced simple geometric shapes. While she is now willing to embrace straighter lines, the pure pleasure she finds in dyeing cloth is unlikely to change.

▲ Rock, Paper, Scissors │ 2001

35 x 45 inches (88.9 x 114.3 cm)
Cotton fabric, rayon thread; hand
dyed, machine pieced and quilted

Photos by Ken Mayer

▲ **Fruition 2: Towards Sunset** | 1999

33 x 44 inches (83.8 x 111.8 cm)
Cotton fabric, rayon thread; hand dyed,
machine pieced and quilted

Photos by Ken Mayer

" I consider my work 'painting with cloth,' but with an
extra tactile element. My quilts are primarily abstract
explorations of form and color and the emotions evoked
by these elements, but I also hope to elicit a physical
response in the viewer. "

▲ **Congregation** | 2004

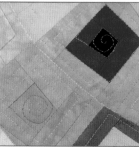

41 x 57 inches (1 x 1.4 m)
Cotton fabric, rayon thread; hand
dyed, machine pieced and quilted

Photos by Ken Mayer

" I work only with cotton fabric I have dyed myself. I don't use fabric made by other artists, because I believe half the creative process of art quilts lies in the creation of the fabrics. Besides immersion dyeing, I sometimes employ surface application techniques, including painting, stamping, screening, and monoprinting. "

▲ **Not Just Another Anita Bryant Day** │ 2001

44 x 34 inches (111.8 x 86.4 cm)
Cotton fabric, rayon thread; hand dyed,
machine pieced and quilted

Photos by Ken Mayer

▲ **Fruition** | 1999

29 x 33 inches (73.7 x 83.8 cm)

Cotton fabric, rayon thread; hand dyed, machine pieced and quilted

Photo by Ken Mayer

▲ **Undercurrents** | 2003

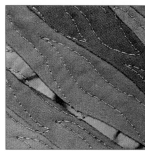

37 x 22 inches
(94 x 55.9 cm)
Cotton fabric, rayon
thread; hand dyed, dye
painted, machine pieced
and quilted

Photos by Ken Mayer

▲ **Recurrent** | 2003

37 x 21 inches (94 x 53.3 cm)
Cotton fabric, rayon thread;
hand dyed, dye painted,
machine pieced and quilted

Photos by Ken Mayer

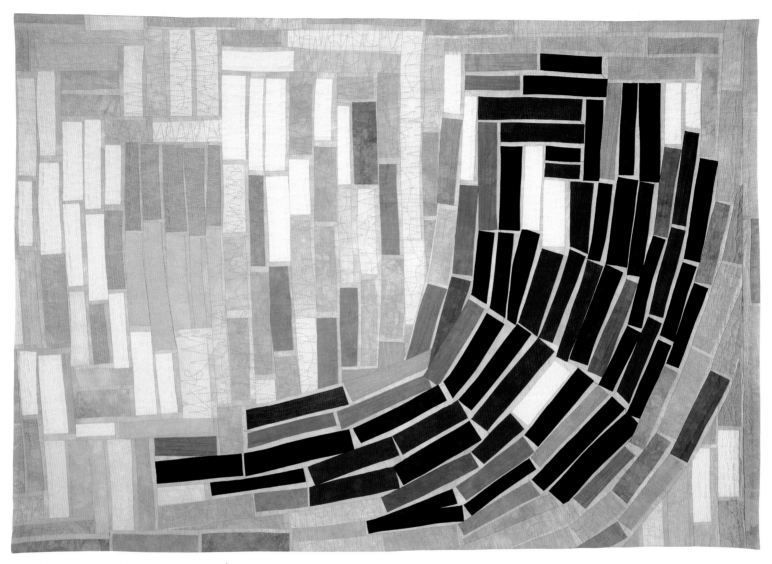

▲ Copia | 2005

38 x 53 inches (96.5 x 134.6 cm)
Cotton; hand dyed, machine
pieced and quilted
Photos by Megan Cartwright

" To be an artist is to grow. My concentration for

several years was the avoidance of the straight

line. My best-known work is composed of curves.

But I have moved and grown, and now embrace

straighter lines. "

▲ **In the Course of This Motion** | 2004

43 x 55 inches (1.1 x 1.4 m)
Cotton fabric, rayon thread; hand dyed,
machine pieced and quilted

Photo by Ken Mayer

▲ My 911 | 2002

35 x 45 inches (88.9 x 114.3 cm)

Cotton fabric, rayon thread; hand dyed, machine pieced and quilted

Photo by Ken Mayer

Noriko Endo

A "DEEP FEELING FOR TREES" is what inspires Noriko Endo. The play of light through the leaves, the changing colors through the seasons, and the strength of a mature trunk all intrigue her. Her technique, which she calls Confetti Naturescapes, allows her to capture the play of light and color she sees during walks in the woods by using tiny pieces of fabric caught under a layer of transparent tulle to create an effect akin to pointillism. Quilting lines may be used to create shadows or to delineate leaves. Her works often incorporate a path meandering through the trees, which seems to invite the viewer to join Endo on her stroll. A spray of spring blossoms or colorful autumn leaves lets the viewer share this Japanese artist's delight in the colors of the seasons. Moreover, it is the particular quality of light coming through the trees that Endo captures best, the creation of a place of mystery and wonder where nature reveals some of her secrets.

▲ **Autumn** | 2005

51 x 49 inches (1.3 x 1.2 m)
Cotton, polyester, tulle; machine quilted, appliquéd and embellished
Photos by Masaru Nomura

▲ **Silent Sentinels** | 2004

66 x 76 inches (1.7 x 1.9 m)
Cotton, tulle; machine quilted,
appliquéd and embellished
Photos by Nagamitsu Endo

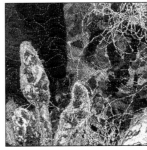

◀ **Chased by the Light** │ 2005

44 x 56 inches (1.1 x 1.4 m)
Cotton, polyester, tulle; machine quilted,
appliquéd and embellished, hand dyed

Photos by Nagamitsu Endo

Sylvan Ambience │ 2006 ▶

78 x 54 inches (2 x 1.4 m)
Cotton, tulle, metallic thread;
machine quilted and
appliquéd, hand painted

Photos by Nagamitsu Endo

NORIKO ENDO

▲ **Autumn in Ohio #2** | 2006

    20 x 24 inches (50.8 x 61 cm)
Cotton, tulle; machine quilted,
appliquéd and embellished
Photos by Masaru Nomura

▲ **Into the Woods** | 2005

25 x 25 inches (63.5 x 63.5 cm)
Cotton, tulle; machine quilted, appliquéd and embellished

Photo by Nagamitsu Endo

▲ Sylvan Ambience #2 | 2006

49 x 60 inches (124.5 x 152.4 cm)
Cotton, polyester, tulle, luminescent fibers;
machine quilted and embroidered

Photos by Brian Blauser

" Trees are a recurring image in my quilts. I believe that a mature tree is one of the boldest graphic impressions that any human will witness in his or her daily life, and my work expresses this theme. "

▲ **Autumn Walk** | 2002

48 x 90 inches (1.2 x 2.3 m)

Cotton, tulle; machine quilted and appliquéd

Photos by Nagamitsu Endo

▲ **Cherry Blossom #3** | 2004

67 x 88 inches (1.7 x 2.2 m)
Cotton, polyester, silk, tulle; machine quilted,
appliquéd and embellished

Photos by Masaru Nomura

▲ **Mother Nature** | 1998

81 x 90 inches (2.1 x 2.3 m)
Cotton, tulle; machine quilted and embellished
Photo by Nagamitsu Endo

Deidre Scherer

I FIRST ENCOUNTERED DEIDRE SCHERER'S WORK at the Brattleboro Museum and Art Center in Vermont. I was overwhelmed by her powerful portrayals of people in varying stages of aging and dying, either alone or surrounded by family and friends. Her portraits are "drawn" three times. She first makes a conventional portrait on paper with pencil, oil pastel, or ink—a process that typically takes two hours. Then she redraws the portrait with scissors without making patterns first, freehand cutting a wide variety of commercial fabrics, whose tiny prints act like pointillist paints. Lastly, she finishes the portrait with lines of zigzag stitching, using the varying widths, colors, and densities of thread to add depth and detail. Scherer says that the aging face serves not only as her subject but as a canvas: Its lines are a portrait of a life. Scherer's portraits show us the beauty that comes from accepting and honoring this important phase of our lives.

▲ **Red Hat** │ 2003

12 x 10 inches (30.5 x 25.4 cm)
Fabric, thread; cut, pieced, layered, machine sewn

Photos by Jeff Baird

Grandchild | 2002 ▶

23 x 19 inches
(58.4 x 48.3 cm)
Fabric, thread; cut,
pieced, layered,
machine sewn

Photo by Jeff Baird

" Through a cyclical progression of cutting, piecing, layering, and machine sewing, I create a tactile surface that actively engages the viewer's eye. Fabric is the perfect vehicle with which to translate elements that are complex, nonverbal, and even invisible. "

◀ Sisters, Too | 1992
23 x 18 inches
(58.4 x 45.7 cm)
Fabric, thread; cut, pieced, layered, machine sewn
Photo by Jeff Baird

" My projects arise as my response to life and to personal experiences. I want my work to initiate a discourse, to encourage thoughtfulness and transformation within our communities. Because of this medium's inherently warm, accessible nature, I see my fabric and thread images cutting through biases and judgments. "

◀ With Patches | 1992

29½ x 19½ inches (74.9 x 49.5 cm)
Fabric, thread; cut, pieced, layered, machine sewn

Photos by Jeff Baird

▲ **Minnie Amalia** | 1982

21¼ x 17¼ inches (54 x 43.8 cm)
Fabric, thread; cut, pieced,
layered, machine sewn

Photo by Jeff Baird

◀ **Listen *from* The Last Year** | 1990

25 x 21 inches (63.5 x 53.3 cm)
Fabric, thread; cut, pieced, layered,
machine sewn, hand sewn, mounted

Photo by Jeff Baird

▲ At Night *from* Surrounded by Family and Friends │ 2000

36 x 48 inches (91.4 x 121.9 cm)

Fabric, thread; cut, pieced, layered, machine sewn

Photo by Jeff Baird

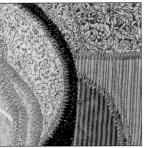

◀ **Woman with Bowl** | 2005

22 x 14 inches
(55.9 x 35.6 cm)
Fabric, thread; cut,
pieced, layered,
machine sewn

Photos by John Polak

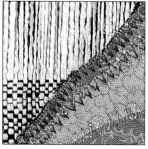

Weaver's Hands | 2005 ▶

15 x 11 inches (38.1 x 27.9 cm)
Fabric, thread, foam-core
board; cut, pieced, layered,
machine sewn over
unraveled cloth

Photos by John Polak

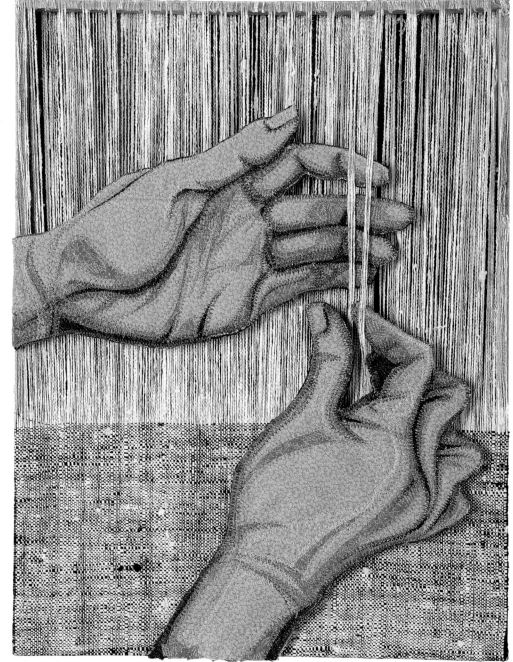

▲ Gifts | 1996

35 x 54 inches (88.9 x 137.2 cm)
Fabric, thread; cut, pieced,
layered, machine sewn

Photo by Jeff Baird

" Fabric stirs our sense of touch, and this awakens a
familiarity that amplifies the visual impact. The texture and
color patterning of printed cloth provide me with points of
color—the same elements found in pointillism and in the
fragmented materials of collage or mosaic. "

Carolyn L. Mazloomi

THREE THEMES ARE PROMINENT in Carolyn L. Mazloomi's work: celebrating women; celebrating jazz and the blues; and abstract work that celebrates her love of color. Her self-taught appliqué style uses fabrics from all over the world. Mazloomi works intuitively. She says the fabrics speak to her, telling her where they want to be placed. Many of her narrative quilts remind women of their power in the role of raising children. Other works record her memories of the treatment African Americans received when she was growing up in the 1950s and during the civil-rights movement. Her music-themed quilts are expressions of joy, celebrations of the music she loves. Recent abstract works experiment with a spontaneous improvisational approach. Founder of the Women of Color Quilters Network in 1985, Mazloomi has worked tirelessly for more than 20 years to create a community of more than 1,700 quilters, networking, educating, curating and promoting exhibitions, and writing books about African-American quilting.

◀ **The Peacekeeper's Gift** | 2006
72 x 54 inches (1.8 x 1.4 m)
Cotton, silk, beads, rayon;
machine appliquéd and quilted
Photos by Robert Giesler

Getting Dizzy | 1998 ▶

52 x 46 inches (1.3 x 1.2 m)
Cotton, silk, netting;
collaged, machine quilted

Photo by Robert Giesler

" My jazz- and blues-themed quilts are my equivalent to making music. The words of a song, the emotion in a singer's voice, or the rhythm of music can inspire a new quilt. Much like the jazz instrumentalist who improvises his music, the quilts have vibes all their own. "

◄ Midnight Jazz | 1999

68 x 52 inches (1.7 x 1.3 m)
Silk, cotton, buttons, beads;
machine appliquéd and quilted

Photo by Frank Giesler

JAZZ ZOOM

CAROLYN L.

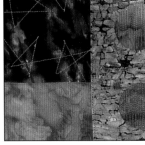

Sticks & Stones Study #4 | 2003 ▶

36 x 29 inches (91.4 x 73.7 cm)
Cotton; appliquéd, machine quilted
Photos by Robert Giesler

▲ **Blues at Annie's Place** | 1997

52 x 70 inches (1.3 x 1.8 m)

Cotton; machine appliquéd, quilted

Photo by Robert Giesler

▲ **In the Winter of My Years
I Can Still See Springtime** | 2000

48½ x 44 inches (1.2 x 1.1 m)
Commercial fabric; appliquéd, machine quilted
Photo by Robert Giesler
Collection of the Rocky Mountain Quilt Museum, Golden, CO

▲ **Wise Woman** | 2000

64 x 50 inches (1.6 x 1.3 m)
Silk, cotton, beads; machine
appliquéd and quilted
Photo by Robert Giesler

▲ Endless Journey | 2000

72 x 57 inches (1.8 x 1.4 m)
Silk, African waxed cotton, beads;
hand dyed, appliquéd and machine quilted

Photo by Robert Giesler

" The spiritual and physical warmth of quilts has always excited me. Quilts are metaphors for love and family, for covering and protecting, for warmth and security. The visual and metaphorical links between textiles and human beings are fertile ground for narrative quilts as statement, and I see myself as a storyteller. "

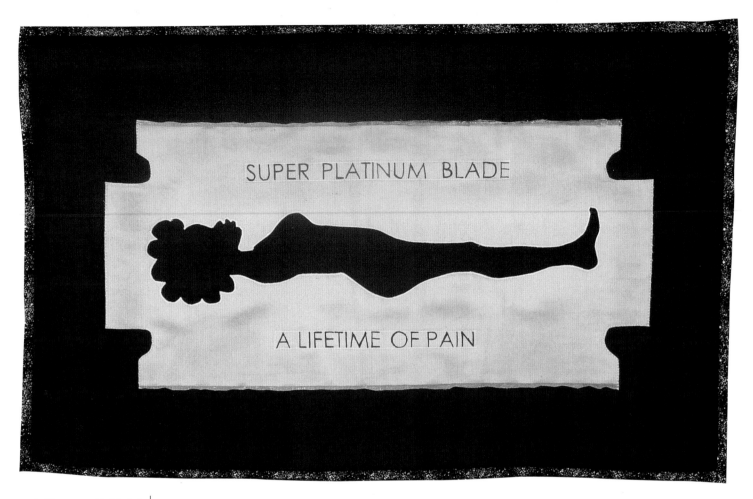

▲ Forever Faithful │ 2004

40 x 67 inches (1 x 1.7 m)
Cotton, acrylic paint; reverse
appliquéd, machine quilted
Photo by Robert Giesler

" Images in my work are not planned but evolve

extemporaneously. My quilts are visual stories that

deal with subject matter that touches my spirit. "

▲ **Seeking Comfort, Finding Pain** | 2006

68 x 54 inches (1.7 x 1.4 m)

Cotton, silk, rayon, beads; machine appliquéd and quilted

Photos by Robert Giesler

Hollis Chatelain

WHAT SHINES THROUGH IN HOLLIS CHATELAIN'S WORK is her love for the people she paints. Based on her own photographs, Chatelain's fiber-reactive dye paintings of her friends from many countries are heavily machine quilted to add shading, depth, and details to the images. Her work in this style began in 1996 and developed out of a deep feeling of homesickness for the people of West Africa, where she lived for 12 years after college. Her yearning for Africa moved her to paint its people, as a way of connecting with them and of sharing her experiences of the joy in their lives. More recent work depicts people from other countries the American artist has visited and has a more direct social agenda, promoting an awareness of the importance of basic human rights: peace, clean drinking water, education, and protection from economic exploitation.

◀ **School: It's Never Too Late to Learn** | 2000

63 x 46 inches (1.6 x 1.2 m)
Cotton fabrics, wool batting,
fiber-reactive dyes; hand dye-
painted, machine quilted

Photos by Lynn Ruck

▲ **A New Day** │ 1998

48 x 45 inches (1.2 x 1.1 m)
African fabrics, cotton batting, cotton, fiber-reactive
dyes; appliquéd, hand dye-painted, machine quilted
Photos by Lynn Ruck

" The 12 years I lived in Africa deeply influenced me. I feel Americans should know more about the joy, harmony, and pride of the African people. "

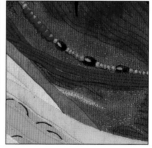

◀ Sahel │ 1997

80 x 60 inches (2 x 1.5 m)
Cotton, cotton/polyester
batting; hand dye-painted,
machine quilted

Photos by Lynn Ruck

HOLLIS CHATELAIN

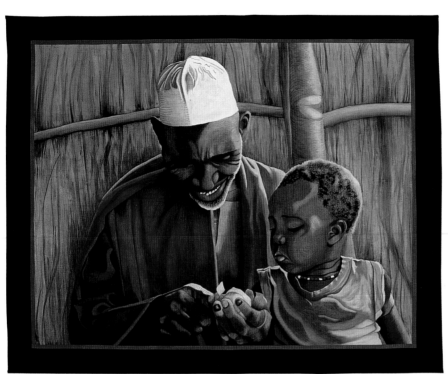

◀ **The Grandfather** | 2000

44 x 54 inches (1.1 x 1.4 m)
Cotton, wool/polyester batting; hand
dye-painted, machine quilted

Photos by Lynn Ruck

Fatima's Son | 2002 ▶

36 x 46 inches (91.4 x 116.8 cm)
Cotton, wool batting; hand dye-
painted, machine quilted

Photos by Lynn Ruck

▲ Tabaski Ram | 1997

    40 x 34 inches (101.6 x 86.4 cm)

    Cotton, cotton classic batting, fiber reactive dyes; hand dye-painted, machine quilted

    Photos by Lynn Ruck

" Much of my work is influenced by personal experiences. I make imagery that evokes an emotional response and creates a mood or atmosphere. My dreams also provide me with an infinite supply of inspiration and reinforce my views and feelings. "

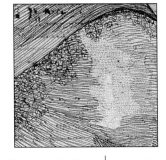

Burkinabe Mother | 2003 ▶

42 x 30 inches (106.7 x 76.2 cm)
Mali cotton fabric, polyester
batting; machine quilted
Photos by Lynn Ruck

▲ **Precious Water** | 2004

    77 x 85 inches (2 x 2.2 m)
    Cotton, polyester batting; hand
    dye-painted, machine quilted
    Photos by Forrest L. Doud

HOLLIS CHATELAIN

▲ **The Gift** | 2006

48 x 53 inches (1.2 x 1.4 m)
Cotton, wool/polyester batting; hand
dye-painted, machine quilted
Photo by Lynn Ruck

▲ **Blue Men** | 2001

60 x 78 inches (1.5 x 2 m)
Cotton, wool batting; hand
dye-painted, machine quilted

Photo by Lynn Ruck

" Since 2000, much of my work has reflected my feelings
about worldwide issues. Whether these concerns are social or
environmental, they have overwhelmed my dreams and manifested
themselves in my art. I would like viewers to see my African imagery
as a tribute to a continent whose people I truly admire and respect. "

Linda Colsh

HER COLORS ARE RESTFUL, but her imagery is not. Linda Colsh's work mostly stays within a limited palette of browns, blacks, and whites. Her imagery explores themes viewers may find somewhat uncomfortable or elegiac: isolation, growing old, invisibility, outrage. Discharge, dye, and paint transform the plain white or black cloth she uses into complex coded messages, where a chair may represent travel and an umbrella indicates isolation. Her pieced background shapes are simple squares and rectangles, yet the surfaces of her work are complex and layered. Her images repeat, fading in and out of the background as if seen through the mist. Figures are mysterious, seemingly glimpsed from a distance. Along with trees, buildings, letters, and maze-like forms, they form irregular patterns across the surface. The viewer has to work to decipher the messages implied in Colsh's imagery, but the resultant sense of a deeper understanding is worth the effort.

▲ Iron Lace | 2006

38 x 39 inches (96.5 x 99.1 cm)
Cotton, used coffee filters, computer images and screens from photography by
the artist; hand dyed, discharged and printed, machine pieced and quilted

Photos by Fotostudio Leemans

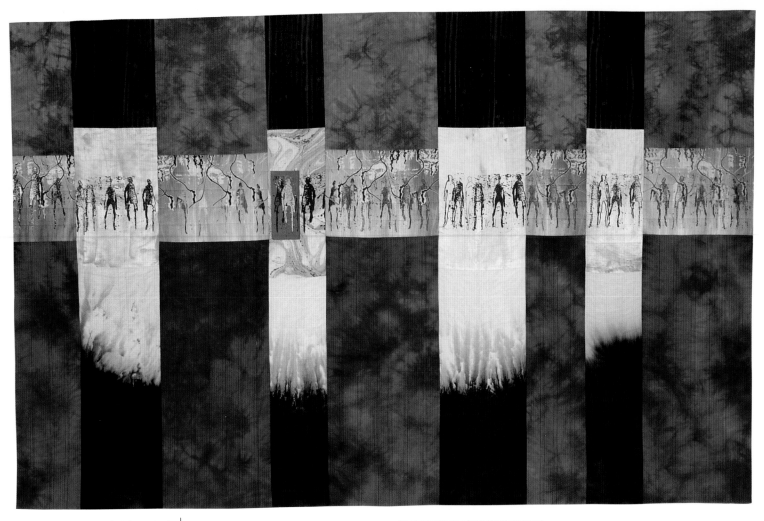

▲ Vanishing Act | 2006

44 x 66 inches (1.1 x 1.7 m)
Cotton, computer images and screens from photography
and drawings by the artist; hand dyed, discharged and
printed, machine pieced and quilted

Photos by Fotostudio Leemans

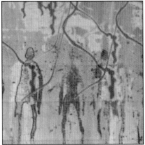

" Surface design is what I enjoy most and what most determines the look of my artwork. As surface design has become the dominant carrier of my message and pattern, the piecework and stitching have become simpler. "

◀ **Northern Renaissance** | 2005

27 x 16 inches (68.6 x 40.6 cm)
Cotton, computer images and screens from photography by the artist; hand dyed and printed, machine pieced and quilted

Photos by Fotostudio Leemans

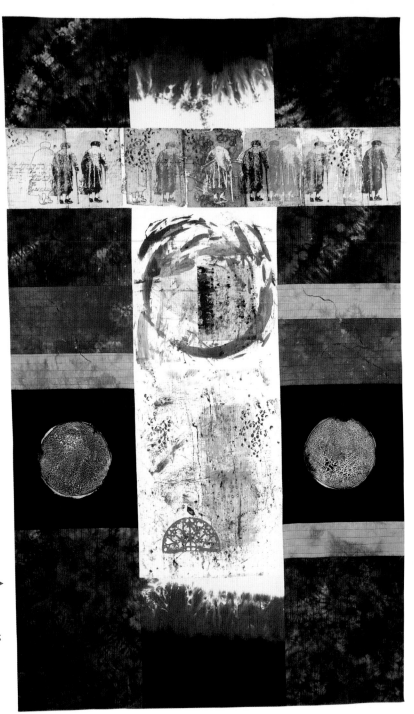

" I distill images into
symbols, packing as
much meaning and
narrative as I can into
a concise icon. I like
images that are both
literal and symbolic, and
words and titles that
have multiple meanings.
My designs employ these
symbols as a personal
iconography. "

The Crack in the Teacup | 2006 ▶

98 x 56 inches (2.5 x 1.4 m)
Cotton fabric, computer images and
screens from photography by the artist;
dyed, discharged, painted, screen-
printed, machine pieced and quilted

Photo by Brian Blauser

de Bron | 2003 ▶

40 x 49 inches (1 x 1.3 m)
Cotton, silk, computer images, stamps
and screens from photography and drawings by the artist; hand dyed, discharged,
painted and printed, machine pieced,
reverse appliquéd and quilted
Photos by Fotostudio Leemans

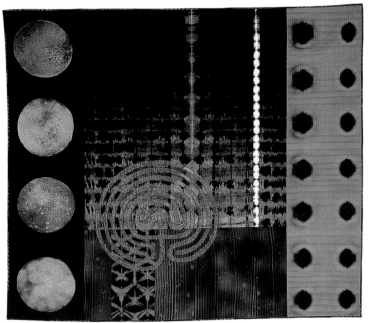

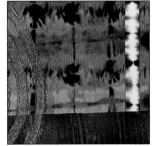

◀ **Mole and Henge** | 2001

56 x 64 inches (1.4 x 1.6 m)
Cotton fabrics, silk-metal organza; hand
discharged and dyed, appliquéd, machine
appliquéd, pieced and quilted
Photos by Fotostudio Leemans

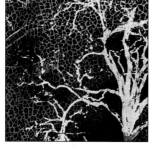

In Winter Woods | 2005 ▶

68 x 48 inches (1.7 x 1.2 m)
Cotton, computer images and
screens from photography by
the artist; hand dyed, discharged and printed, machine
pieced and quilted

Photos by Fotostudio Leemans

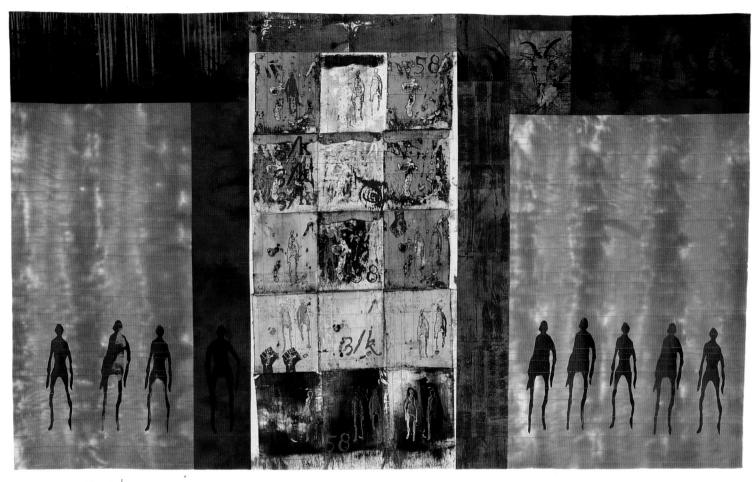

▲ **Memory Shed** | 2006

43 x 70 inches (1.1 x 1.8 m)
Cotton, computer images and
screens from photography and
drawings by the artist; hand
dyed, printed, machine pieced
and quilted

Photo by Fotostudio Leemans

" While I express ideas in my art quilts, I don't want to explain everything. There should be some blanks to fill in, a little mystery, some fog. Content is important; however, I want viewers to pause, receive the impression I put forward, and then derive something for themselves. "

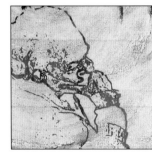

▲ **Drift** | 2006

57 x 52 inches (1.5 x 1.3 m)
Cotton, computer images and screens from photography and drawings by
the artist; hand dyed, discharged and printed, machine pieced and quilted

Photos by Fotostudio Leemans

▲ **Culture (Day Lilies)** | 2007

26 x 33 inches (66 x 83.8 cm)
Cotton, computer images and screens from photography and drawings by the artist; hand dyed,
painted and printed, machine pieced and quilted

Photos by Fotostudio Leemans

Charlotte Yde

"ARTWORK IS THE PHYSICAL EVIDENCE of emotional states," says Danish artist Charlotte Yde. She works in series that express these different emotional states while she explores her constantly expanding list of "What if?" questions. Her pieced forms are simple in design, but they use a wide variety of surface design techniques to convey the profound symbolic messages hidden within her designs. Many of Yde's works explore themes of history, especially the history of war, using design elements that include crosses, shields, broken vessels, and Vikings. Other works focus on the beauty of gardens or the variations found in people's personalities. The rust series is about time, both symbolically and literally. Yde says the rusting takes a long time and forces her to be more patient with the process than she usually is, but she also says that "sometimes you have to listen to what the fabrics tell you to do."

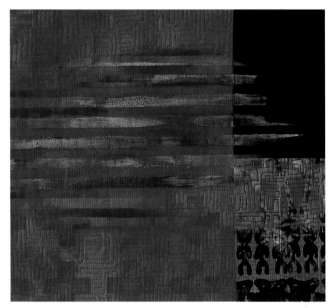

▲ Bloody Garden | 2002

  44 x 52 inches (1.1 x 1.3 m)
  Hand-dyed and commercial cotton; dyed,
  painted, machine pieced and quilted

  Photos by Niels Jensen

◀ **The Writing on the Wall** | 2001

33 x 24 inches (83.8 x 61 cm)
Hand-dyed and commercial
cotton, silk/metallic organza;
screen-printed, layered, machine
pieced and quilted

Photos by artist

Red Horizon Line | 1995 ▶

59 x 45 inches (1.5 x 1.2 m)
Hand-dyed and commercial
cotton; machine pieced
and quilted

Photos by Dennis Rosenfeldt

▲ Feeling Blue | 1995

    45 x 43 inches (1.2 x 1.1 m)
Hand-dyed and commercial cotton;
machine pieced and quilted

Photo by Dennis Rosenfeldt

▲ Japanese Garden | 2002

43 x 48 inches (1.1 x 1.2 m)
Old Japanese kimono fabric, hand-printed and commercial silk
and cotton; rust printed, machine pieced and quilted
Photo by Dennis Rosenfeldt

" I didn't start out making traditional quilts. Rather, I saw quilt-making as a challenging and natural artistic medium. Today, inspiration for my work can come from many sources: journeys, colors, fabrics, certain ideas, or concepts. "

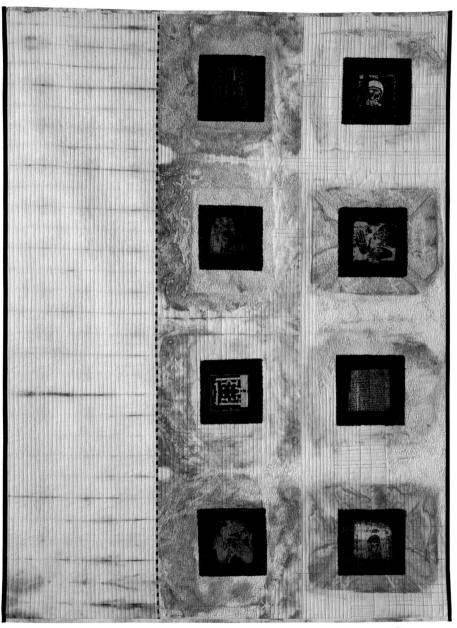

▲ **Secrets of the Desert** | 2004
58 x 43 inches (1.5 x 1.1 m)
Cotton; rust printed, machine pieced and quilted
Photos by Niels Jensen

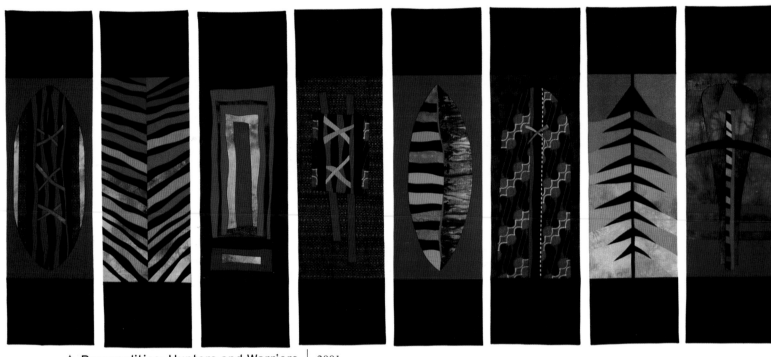

▲ **Personalities–Hunters and Warriors** | 2001

59 x 148 inches (1.5 x 3.8 m)
Hand-dyed and commercial cotton;
machine pieced and quilted

Photo by Dennis Rosenfeldt

" I mainly work in series, because that's
what feels natural to me. It allows me
to go in-depth with certain aspects of
the work. However, I find it very hard
to be confined by overly strict rules and
regulations for too long, so I tend to shift
between different series. "

▲ **Personalities–Feeling Blue** | 2001

53 x 69 inches (1.4 x 1.8 m)
Cotton, silk/metallic organza; layered,
machine pieced and quilted

Photo by Dennis Rosenfeldt

" Journeys have been a big part of my life, and from time to time they have led me astray, to detours from the route I planned. Journeys have often influenced my quiltmaking. My quilts reflect both inner and outer travels. "

Imprints of Time I | 2004–2005 ▲
68 x 55 inches (1.7 x 1.4 m)
Cotton sateen, cotton; rust printed,
machine pieced and quilted
Photos by Niels Jensen

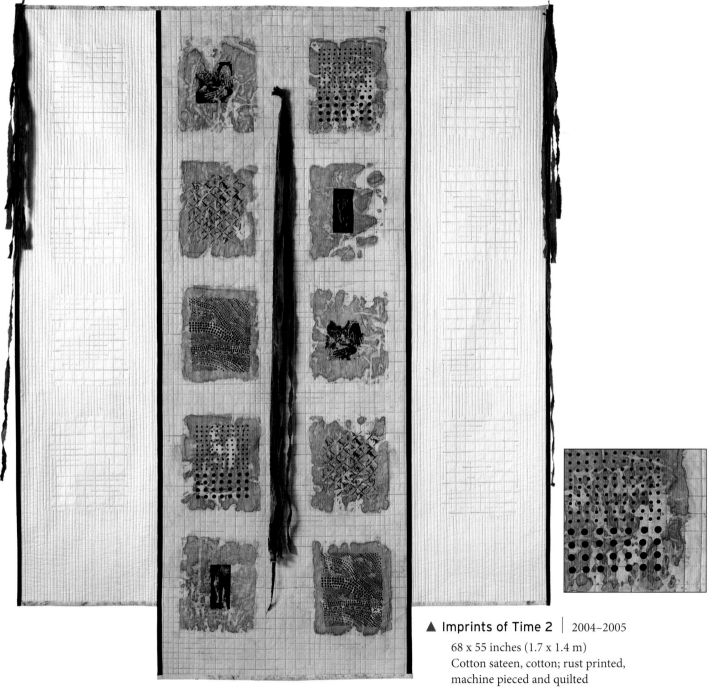

▲ **Imprints of Time 2** | 2004–2005

68 x 55 inches (1.7 x 1.4 m)
Cotton sateen, cotton; rust printed,
machine pieced and quilted

Photos by Niels Jensen

Joan Schulze

COMBINING PHOTOGRAPHY, PRINTING, various transfer processes, and collage, Joan Schulze's work interprets her life like a series of visual journal entries. Layers of translucent fabric, fragments of transferred photos, and bits of monoprinted cloth are joined to offer an elusive sense of shifting meanings. Her description of the genesis of her tea-bowl series seems typical—in the process of photographing her collection of Japanese tea bowls for cataloguing, she became so interested in the images that she made a series of art quilts with them rather than finishing the catalog. The resulting works honor the tea bowl's simple yet elegant form and also its importance in traditional Japanese society as an object that is beautiful in part because of its utility. Often combined with her own poetry, Schulze's work creates a sense of déjà vu—a feeling that if you could only see the images more clearly, you could remember, too.

▲ Thirteen Bowls | 2002

21¼ x 24¼ inches (54 x 61.6 cm)
Cotton, paper, silk; direct printed, monoprinted,
pieced, machine stitched and quilted

Photos by Sharon Risedorph

▲ **Shoes** | 1998

44 x 42 inches (1.1 x 1.1 m)
Silk, paper, cotton; photo transferred, monoprinted, painted,
appliquéd, pieced, machine stitched and quilted

Photo by Sharon Risedorph

" From the beginning of my artistic journey I used text in embroidery, quilts, and collage. I have been greatly influenced by illuminated manuscripts. In that spirit, I may add complex marks, playful drawings unrelated to the text or subject, or metal leaf to my quilts. "

▲ Blue Notes | 2003

27¼ x 25¼ inches (69.2 x 64.1 cm)

Silk, paper, cotton; photo transferred, pieced, machine and hand stitched

Photo by Sharon Risedorph

◀ **Forest—Bamboo and Moss** │ 2000

44 x 11 inches (111.8 x 27.9 cm)
Silk, paper, cotton; photo transferred,
monoprinted, machine quilted

Photos by Sharon Risedorph

Forest—By the River │ 2000 ▶

44 x 11 inches (111.8 x 27.9 cm)
Silk, paper, cotton; photo
transferred, monoprinted, machine
quilted

Photos by Sharon Risedorph

" Erasures, fragments, and layering are my primary processes. Discarded and unattractive found materials are often juxtaposed with silk, paper, and cotton, which I have altered using paint, photocopy, and glue-transfer methods. I find things are more interesting to me if they are elusive and poetic. "

▲ Domino Theory | 2001
47½ x 48 inches (1.2 x 1.2 m)
Silk, paper, cotton; photo transferred, pieced,
reverse appliquéd, machine stitched and quilted
Photos by Sharon Risedorph

" The how and the why of my work have changed radically as I've discovered new methods and changed themes or materials. My latest discovery is toner drawings on silk. Over time I have improvised ways of putting copies onto cloth. The immediacy of this method allows a rapid processing of images and ideas. "

Currents | 2002 ▶

70 x 47½ inches (1.8 x 1.2 m)
Cotton, silk, paper; photo and glue transferred, monoprinted, machine stitched and quilted

Photos by Sharon Risedorph

▲ Tea House | 2002

21¼ x 23¾ inches (54 x 60.3 cm)
Silk; direct printed, monoprinted, painted,
pieced, machine stitched and quilted

Photos by Sharon Risedorph

▲ **Dancing Lessons** | 2006

39½ x 39¾ inches (1 x 1 m)
Silk, toner drawing; direct photocopy
printed, machine quilted

Photo by Sharon Risedorph

▲ **Private Dreams of the Writer** | 2005–2006

    42 x 54 inches (1.1 x 1.4 m)
    Cotton, silk, paper; monoprinted, photocopy and
    glue transferred, machine pieced and quilted

    Photos by Sharon Risedorph

Judith Content

THE PLAY OF LIGHT OVER WATER is what inspires Judith Content's work and gives it a peaceful, reminiscent quality. Often constructed in an irregular shape that looks like a simplified kimono, the work uses a contemporary approach to the traditional Japanese dye technique of *arashi-shibori*. Content's *arashi-shibori* resist process of pleating, wrapping, discharging, and over-dyeing black silk produces markings reminiscent of wind-driven rain or lapping waves. It's a long, slow process, which Content says leaves her much time for thinking about each piece. The slanting patterns of her fabrics express Content's lifelong fascination with water in all its

forms—inlets, coastal marshes, fog—to produce a happy marriage of form and inspiration. Content takes her direction for each piece from the fabrics produced by that work's dye session. The fabrics are then cut, torn, rearranged, sewn together, and quilted to convey the mood of a memory of a place. Judith Content became the president of Studio Art Quilt Associates in 2007.

◀ **Tule Fog** | 2006

79 x 65 inches (2 x 1.7 m)
Silk charmeuse; shibori dyed, discharged,
machine pieced and quilted

Photos by James Dewrance

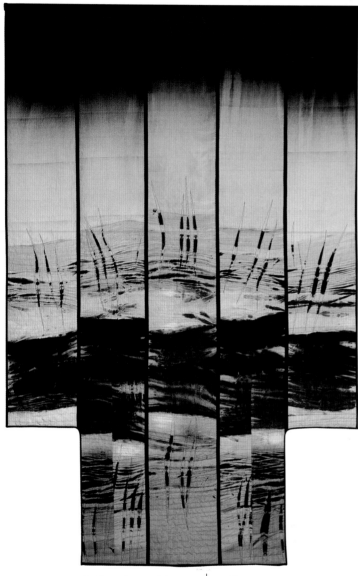

▲ **Sumie and Snow** | 2003

79 x 50 inches (2 x 1.3 m)
Black Thai silk; shibori dyed,
discharged, pieced, quilted,
appliquéd

Photo by James Dewrance

Tempest | 2000 ▶

88 x 52 inches (2.2 x 1.3 m)
Thai silk; shibori dyed,
discharged, pieced, quilted

Photo by artist

" My background in watercolor painting and my love of building things led naturally to the construction of quilts. Every aspect of my work, from the dyeing to the piecing to the quilting and appliqué, relies on intuition as well as experience. "

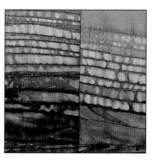

◀ **Still Water** | 2005

71 x 30 inches (180.3 x 76.2 cm)
Thai silk; shibori dyed, discharged, pieced, quilted, appliquéd
Photos by James Dewrance

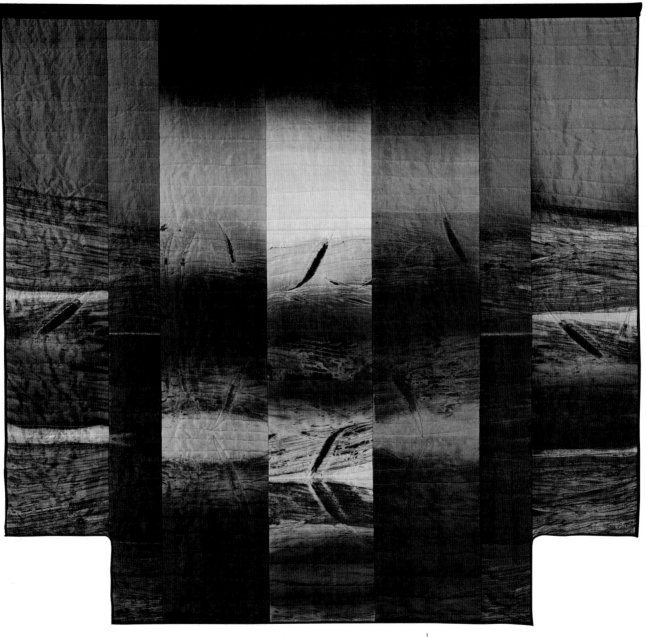

▲ **Leaves Fall, Feathers Float, Fish Swim Upstream** | 1999

61 x 58 inches (1.6 x 1.5 m)
Black Thai silk; shibori dyed, discharged, pieced, quilted

Photo by James Dewrance

▲ **Luminaria** | 1998

59 x 68 inches (1.5 x 1.7 m)
Thai silk; shibori dyed, discharged, pieced, quilted

Photo by Richard Johns

▲ **Sweltering Sky Kimono** | 1992
61 x 52 inches (1.6 x 1.3 m)
Silk satin; shibori dyed, discharged,
pieced, quilted, appliquéd
Photo by James Dewrance

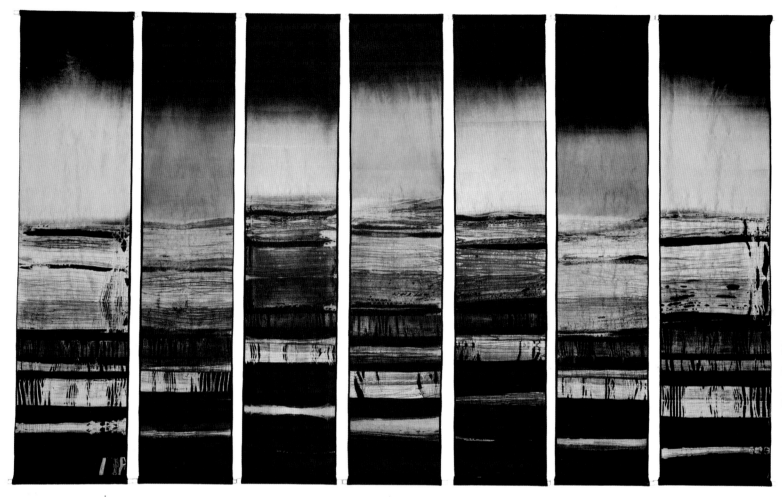

▲ **Calligraphy** | 1998

Largest panels, 59 x 10½ inches (149.9 x 26.7 cm);
smallest panels, 59 x 12½ inches (149.9 x 31.8 cm)
Thai silk; shibori dyed, discharged, pieced, quilted

Photos by Richard Johns

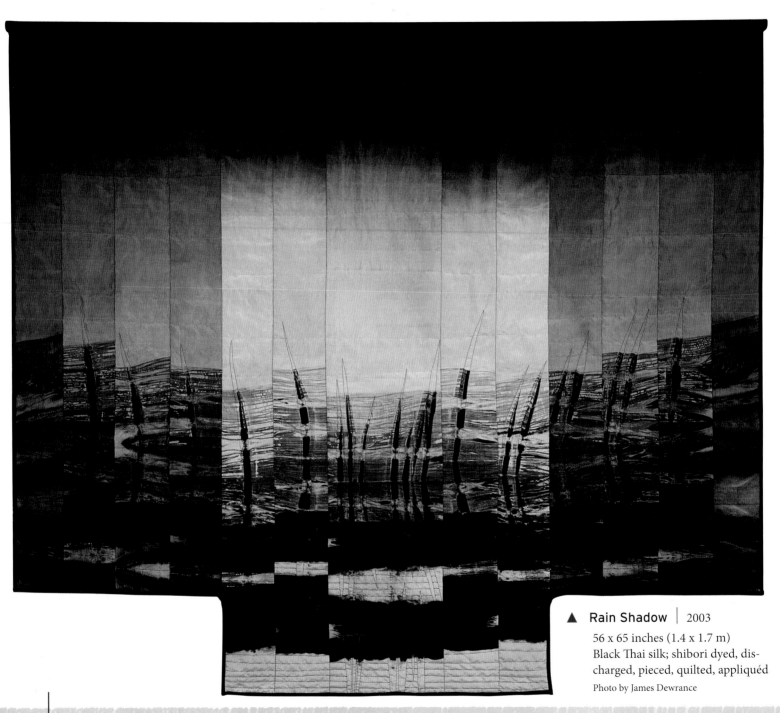

▲ **Rain Shadow** | 2003

56 x 65 inches (1.4 x 1.7 m)

Black Thai silk; shibori dyed, discharged, pieced, quilted, appliquéd

Photo by James Dewrance

Chasm | 2006 ▶

86 x 46 inches (2.2 x 1.2 m)
Thai silk; shibori dyed, discharged,
pieced, quilted, appliquéd

Photos by James Dewrance

" Like haiku, my work explores the essence of an image or a moment in time. I find inspiration in nature's waterways, from estuaries to desert pools. Just as haiku often have different interpretations, I hope that the meditative quality of my pieces encourages viewers to draw upon their own memories and experiences when contemplating my work. "

Kyoung Ae Cho

REPETITION OF NATURAL FORMS characterizes the work of Kyoung Ae Cho, who was born in South Korea and now teaches at the University of Wisconsin–Milwaukee. She is especially drawn to the linear qualities of trees, wood grains, and leaves, partly as visual statements but also as marks of a tree's natural rhythm and history. Gathering and collecting materials to use in her work is like a ceremony that begins what Cho sees as a collaboration between herself and nature. While Cho makes much of her work as sculpture, she references quilting in her pieces through form and through the encasing of natural elements within layers of sheer fabric. Stitching is used for structural purposes—to attach pieces of wood to a backing—or for decorative ends, to echo the repeating lines of the leaf forms. Cho's foremost interest is in rendering the chaos of nature. But her work also seeks to bring order and a sense of pattern to the natural forms she presents for our contemplation.

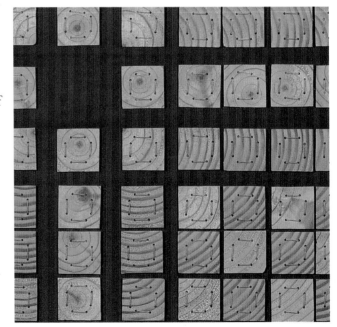

▲ Quilt?!-I | 1997

54 x 54 inches (1.4 x 1.4 m)

Wood, fabric, waxed linen cord, thread; sliced, drilled, sewn

Photos by artist

" My investigation into environmental processing explores nature's rhythm in our culture and how we interact with nature. My works are produced as a result of an ongoing conversation between myself and nature. Collecting objects and materials is essential to my working process. "

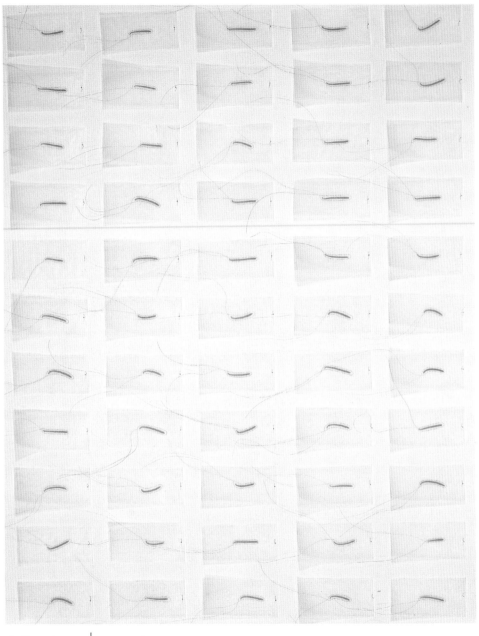

▲ **Specimen** | 2002

119 x 28 inches (302.3 x 71.1 cm)
Balsam fir needles, hair, silk organza, pins; hand stitched
Photo by artist

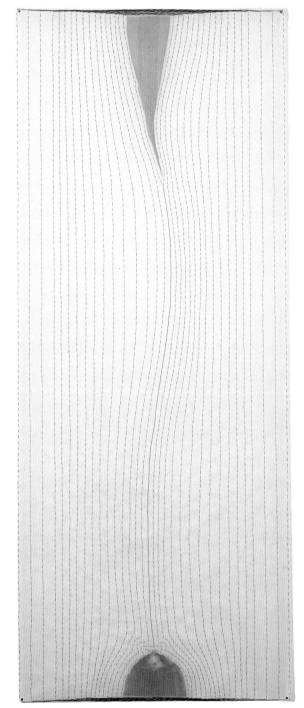

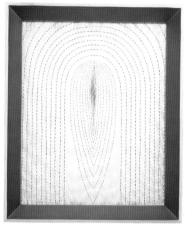

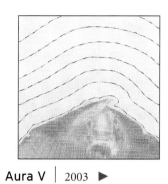

Aura V | 2003 ▶

Each section, 11⅛ x 9⅛ x 1¾ inches (28.2 x 23.2 x 4.4 cm)
Grass, silk organza, thread, frame; hand stitched

Photos by artist

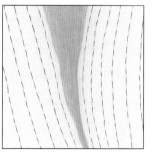

◀ **Connected** | 2006

27¾ x 11 inches (70.5 x 27.9 cm)
Corn leaves, silk organza, thread; hand stitched

Photos by artist

KYOUNG AE

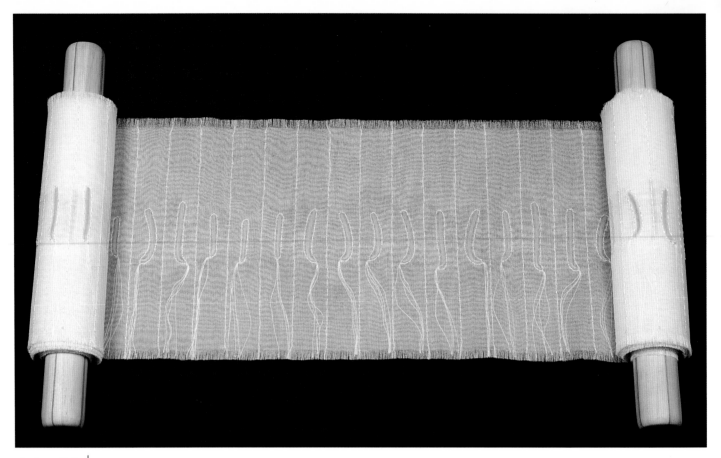

▲ **Scroll II** | 2000

Open, 9 x 142 inches (22.9 x 360.7 cm)
Balsam fir needles, silk organza, thread,
wood; hand stitched

Photos by artist

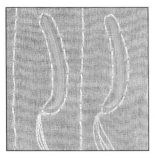

**" I respectfully approach environmental processing
by incorporating recycled matter as well as low-
valued, man-made materials into my work. In the
process, I examine nature and its changes in order
to understand the elements of its language: shape,
pattern, color, texture, scale. "**

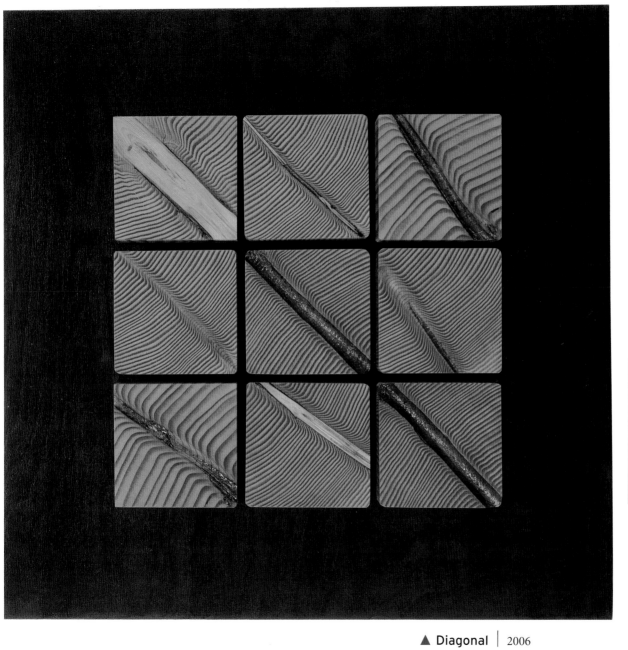

▲ **Diagonal** | 2006

21 x 21 inches (53.3 x 53.3 cm)
Wood; sliced

Photos by artist

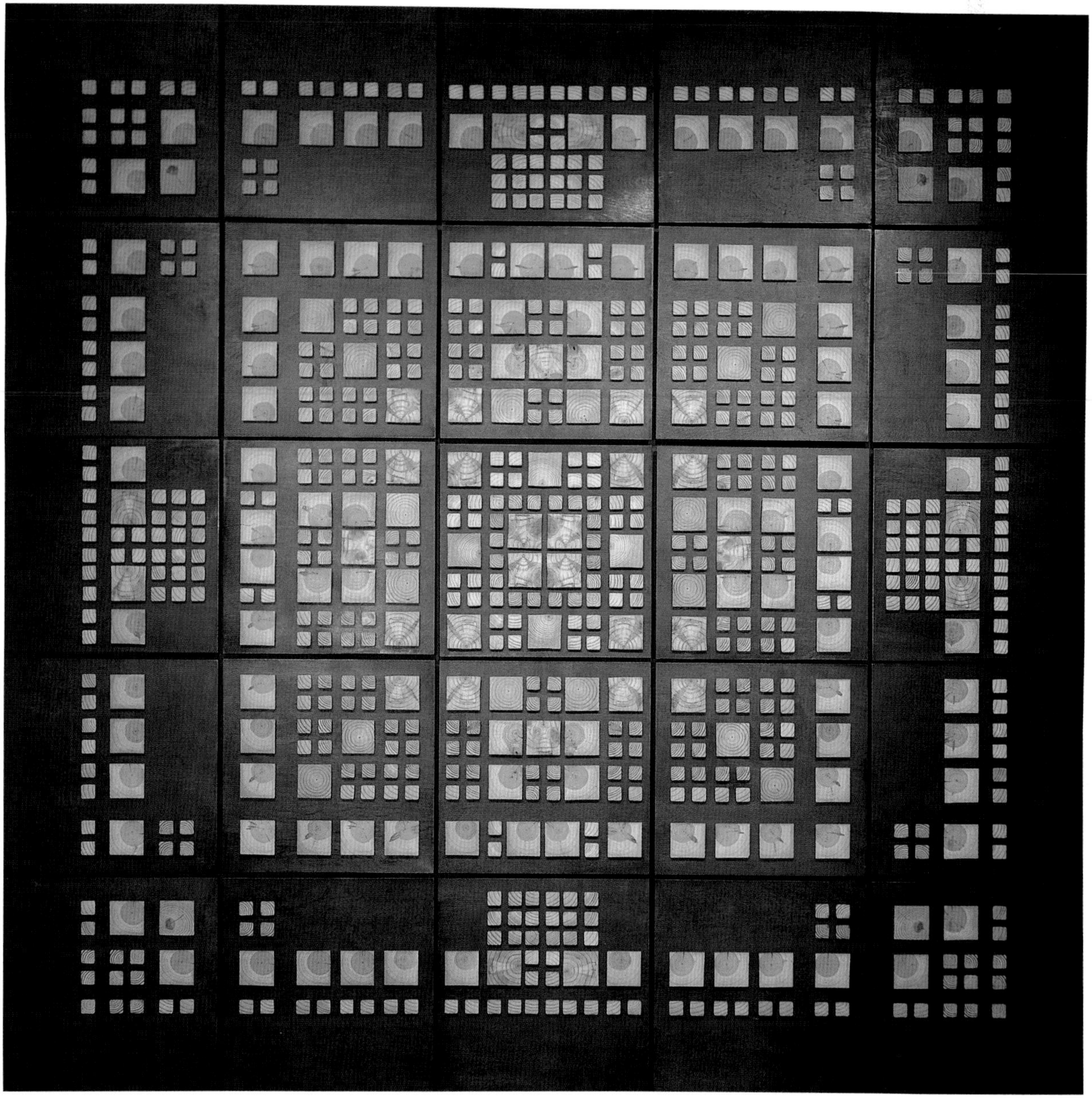

▲ **Reconfigured** | 2007

109½ x 109½ inches (2.8 x 2.8 m)
Wood; sliced, drilled, sanded, stained

Photo by artist

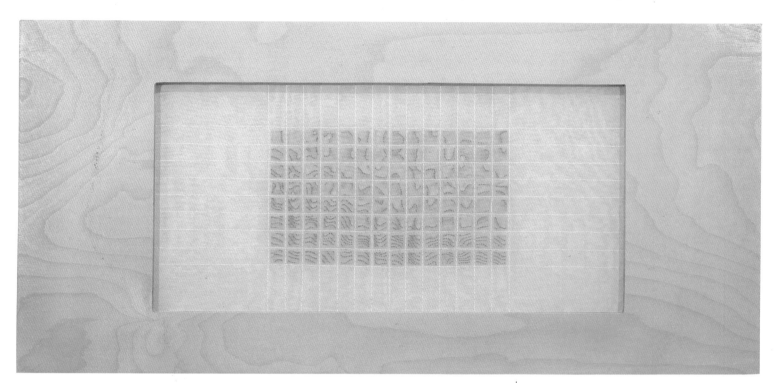

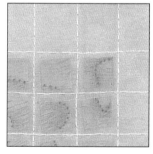

▲ Landscape I | 2000
14 x 30 inches (35.6 x 76.2 cm)
Wood, silk organza, thread;
sliced, burned, hand stitched
Photos by artist

" My creative research has been based on beauty in nature—exploring the idea of pattern-making, incorporating and borrowing patterns in nature, and harmonizing natural and man-made materials. While working on my pieces, I also think of the harmony between the natural and the man-made, the spiritual and the physical. "

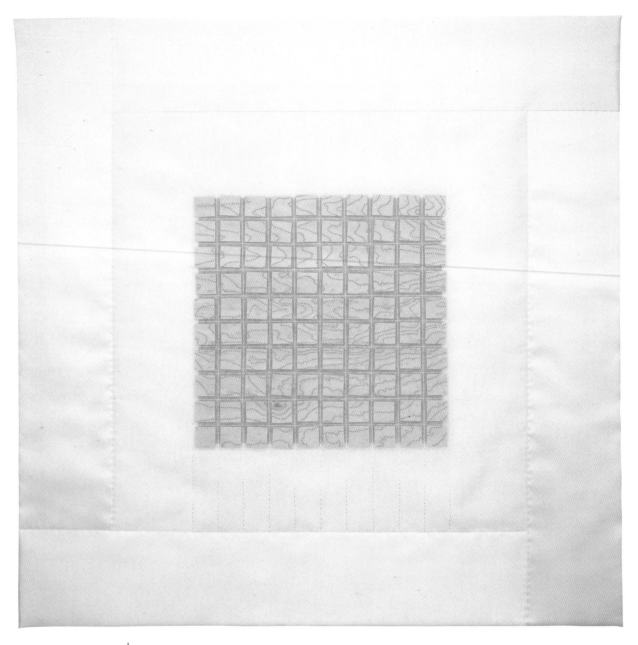

▲ InnerScape III │ 2000

30 x 30 inches (76.2 x 76.2 cm)
Maple veneer, silk organza, silk satin organza, thread; burned, hand stitched, sewn
Photo by artist

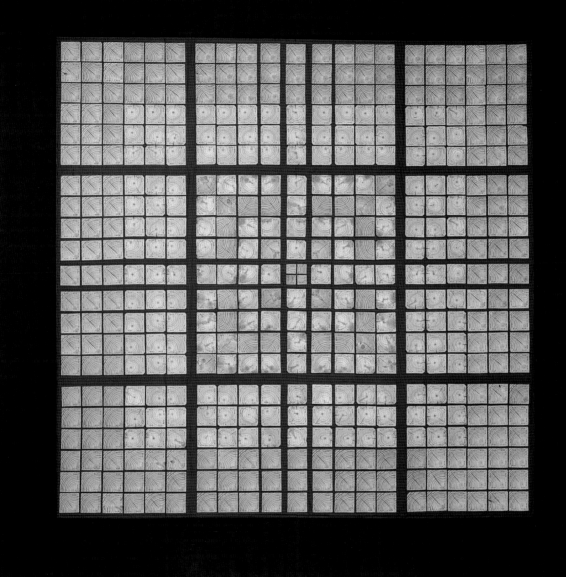

▲ Aged, Covered by Wisdom | 1996

108 x 108 inches (2.7 x 2.7 m)

Wood, fabric, waxed linen cord, thread; sliced, drilled, sewn

Photo by artist

Jette Clover

THE RELATIONSHIP BETWEEN TIME, MEMORY, and language is what fascinates Jette Clover. A Dane by birth, Clover has a background in journalism and has lived in several countries. She speaks several languages, and much of her work is concerned with a hunt for traces of human communication. Indecipherable faded writing, fragments of maps and photos, and repeated X marks are collaged into her pieces. Much of her work is monochromatic, because she finds that concentrating on one color increases the psychological and symbolic associations the viewer has with that color, even as it creates a greater emphasis on the piece's textures. Cheesecloth is a common element in her work because it can be colored yet remain transparent, allowing glimpses of the layers beneath. Using a variety of different methods to alter her fabrics, from dyeing and painting to photo transfer and rusting, Clover takes fragments of the results and layers them. Her compositions seem to convey a message that is almost tauntingly within reach, yet still elusive.

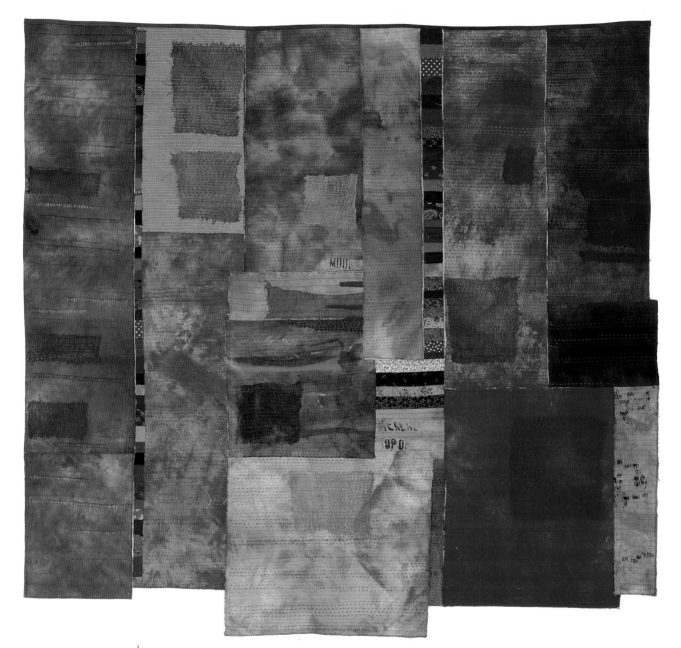

▲ Red Color Field | 2007

55 x 58 inches (1.4 x 1.5 m)
Hand-dyed cotton, linen, cheesecloth; hand and machine quilted, collaged

Photos by Pol Leemans

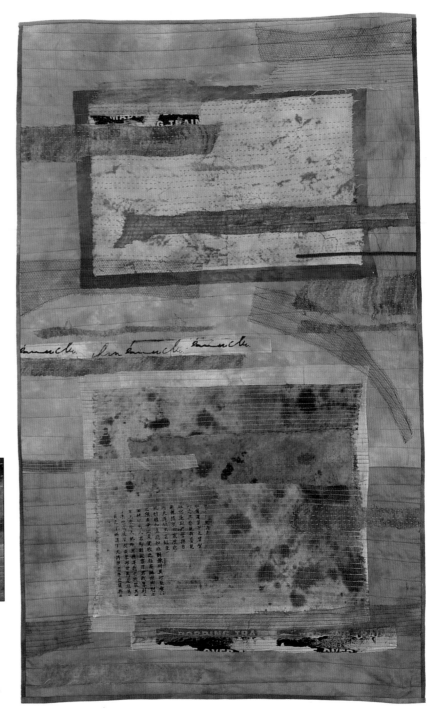

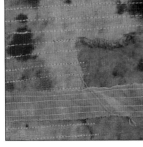

Blue Landscape | 2004 ▶

46 x 28 inches (116.8 x 71.1 cm)
Cotton, linen and cheesecloth,
netting; hand dyed, screen-printed,
hand and machine quilted, collaged

Photos by Pol Leemans

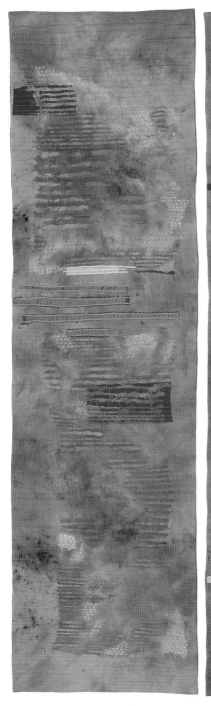

" I am inspired by the passing of time, by the traces we leave behind in our surroundings. I am not scratching my name on an ancient cathedral wall, nor am I spray-painting a railroad car to verify my presence. I have chosen to leave my markings with stitches on cloth. I make quilts. "

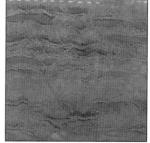

◀ **Yellow Companions** | 2002

58 x 33 inches (147.3 x 83.8 cm)
Cotton, cheesecloth, silk; hand dyed, slashed, hand and machine quilted, collaged

Photos by Pol Leemans

" The use of recycled
pieces of clothing
and the transfer of
handwriting onto fabric
help me tell my stories
of that which has come
before. It makes me
remember the people
and places that have
shaped my life. "

▲ **Transition I** | 2002

32 x 29 inches (81.3 x 73.7 cm)
Cotton, cheesecloth, silk, paper; hand dyed, painted, screen-
printed, machine pieced, hand quilted, collaged

Photo by Pol Leemans

JETTE CLOVER

▲ Small Notes #100, Greta Garbo │ 2006

    7 x 6 inches (17.8 x 15.2 cm)
    Cotton, silk, cheesecloth; collaged, hand quilted
    Photo by Pol Leemans

▲ Memento #17 │ 2001

    8 x 6 inches (20.3 x 15.2 cm)
    Hand-dyed and commercial cotton;
    screen-printed, photo transferred,
    hand quilted, collaged
    Photos by artist

JETTE CLOVER

" The basic element of a quilt is layering, literally and spiritually. Making a quilt is a building process—layers of fabric and layers of memories, hopes, and dreams stitched together. Visible and invisible seams. Stitch by stitch, in and out through the fabric in a similar repetitive rhythm as moving a pen across paper. "

JETTE CLOVER

Silent Music | 2002 ▶

57 x 43 inches (1.5 x 1.1 m)
Cotton and cheesecloth;
hand dyed, screen-printed,
slashed, hand and machine
quilted, collaged

Photo by Pol Leemans

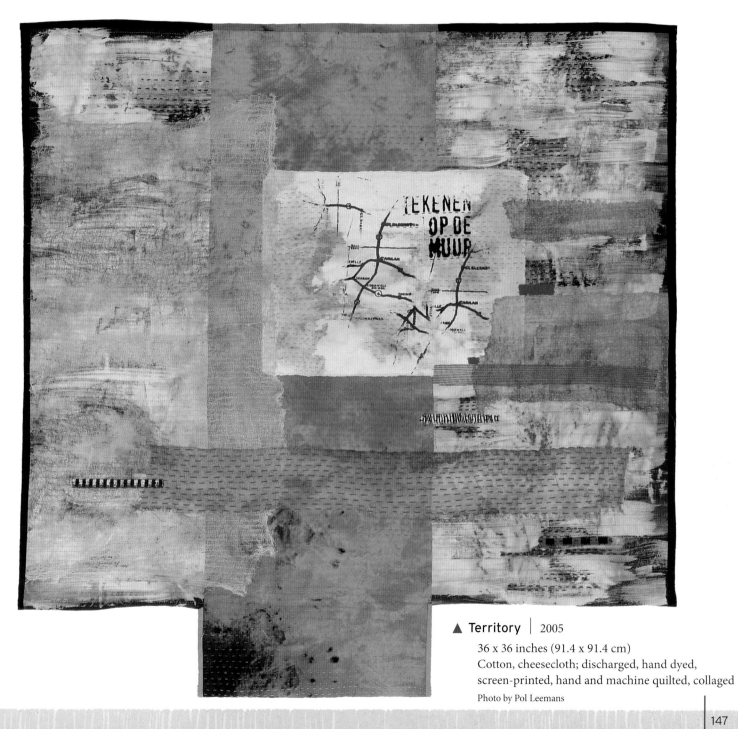

▲ **Territory** | 2005

36 x 36 inches (91.4 x 91.4 cm)
Cotton, cheesecloth; discharged, hand dyed,
screen-printed, hand and machine quilted, collaged

Photo by Pol Leemans

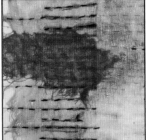

▲ **Green Cross** | 2006

26 x 23 inches (66 x 58.4 cm)
Cotton, cheesecloth; hand dyed, rusted, screen-
printed, hand and machine quilted, collaged

Photos by Pol Leemans

▲ **The Sea at Midday** │ 1999

37 x 40 inches (94 x 101.6 cm)

Cotton, netting, polyester, dye; hand dyed, machine pieced, hand quilted, collaged

Photo by artist

Eszter Bornemisza

A DOCTORATE IN MATHEMATICS may have contributed to Eszter Bornemisza's lifelong interest in looking for and finding patterns in the world around her. Seeing the web of fabric as akin to the web of life created by human settlement, in her intricately appliquéd works in an earthy palette of reds and browns, Bornemisza celebrates the spirit of the people who built settlements and pathways long ago. Bornemisza's early works were pieced from over-dyed commercial fabrics, but her more recent quilts feature collage, which allows the Hungarian artist to work more spontaneously. She uses torn and frayed fabrics to express the sense of decay and dissolving patterns she sees. Often resembling aerial photos or geological layers, Bornemisza's works present fabric fragments and markings for contemplation. In our time of computer mathematical modeling of human interaction, the reconciliation of these patterns of people and cloth may be closer than ever.

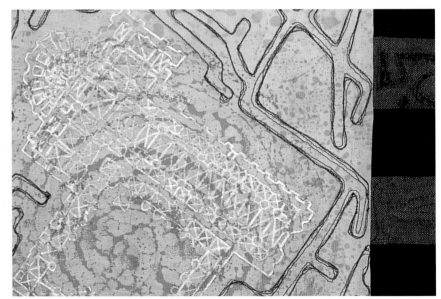

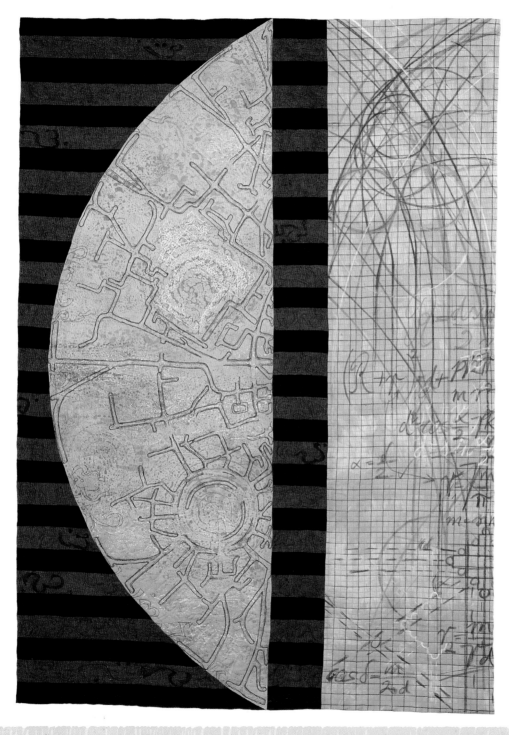

◀ **Foundation** | 2006

64 x 44 inches (1.6 x 1.1 m)
Cotton; monoprinted, drawn, dyed,
printed, pieced, machine quilted

Photos by Pál Csillag

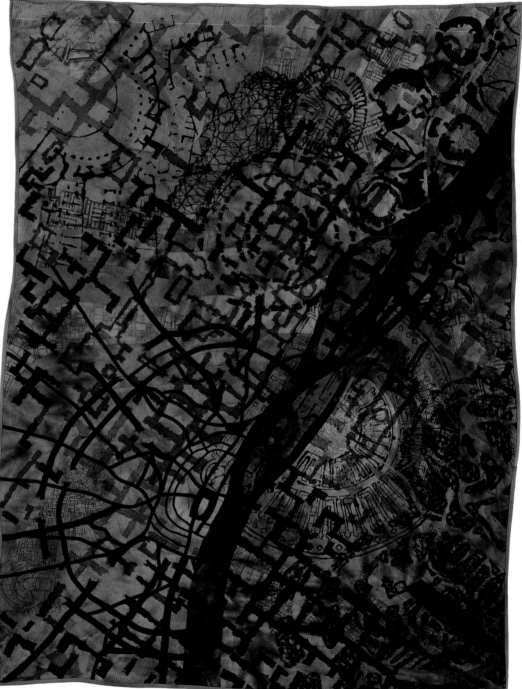

" My main sources of
inspiration are the
layers of history and
age in the earth—signs
and traces of the past,
and their meanings
for us. For inspiration,
I like to use maps of
ancient settlements and
dwellings that preserve
the spirit of the people
who lived there. "

ESZTER BORNEMISZA

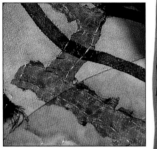

Layers | 2001 ▶
48 x 36 inches
(121.9 x 91.4 cm)
Cotton, hot-cut synthetics;
dyed, collaged, machine
quilted
Photos by Tihanyi-Bakos

▲ **Course of Time** │ 2006

40 x 40 inches (1 x 1 m)
Whole-cloth cotton, linen, silk, hot-cut synthetics; wax-resist
painted, dyed, frayed, machine appliquéd and quilted

Photos by Aron Levendel

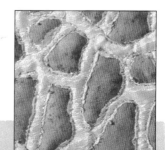

▲ **Cosmic Embrace** | 1999

54 x 64 inches (1.4 x 1.6 m)
Overdyed commercial cotton; painted, pieced, machine quilted
Photo by Tihanyi-Bakos

◀ Longing for Africa | 2004

60 x 48 inches (1.5 x 1.2 m)
Overdyed commercial cotton,
hot-cut synthetics; discharged,
dyed, collaged, machine quilted

Photos by Tihanyi-Bakos

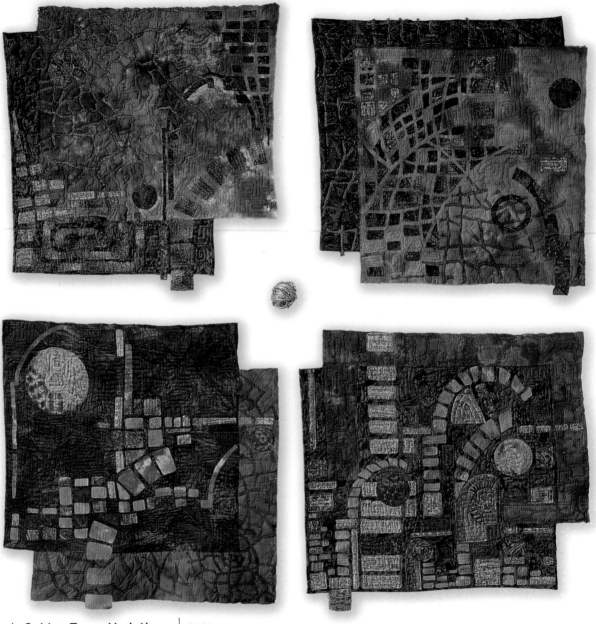

▲ Golden Town–Variations | 2004

64 x 64 inches (1.6 x 1.6 m)
Cotton, hot-cut synthetics; dyed, fused, positive and
negative appliquéd, machine quilted

Photo by Tihanyi-Bakos

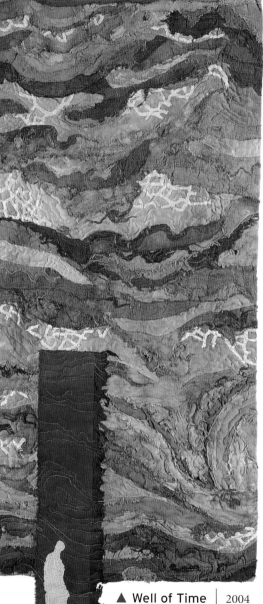

▲ **Well of Time** | 2004

66 x 28 inches (167.6 x 71.1 cm)
Cotton, wool, hot-cut synthetics,
paper; dyed, frayed, felted, collaged,
machine quilted

Photo by Tihanyi-Bakos

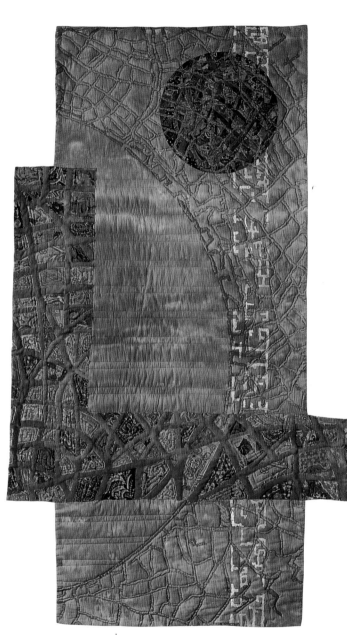

▲ **Siena** | 2005

64 x 36 inches (162.6 x 91.4 cm)
Cotton, hot-cut synthetics; dyed, fused,
collaged, machine quilted

Photo by Tihanyi-Bakos

ESZTER BORNEMISZA

▲ Fragments of the Past │ 2004

30 x 36 inches (76.2 x 91.4 cm)
Whole-cloth cotton, wool, hot-cut
synthetics; wax-resist painted, felted,
machine quilted

Photos by Tihanyi-Bakos

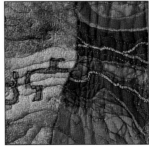

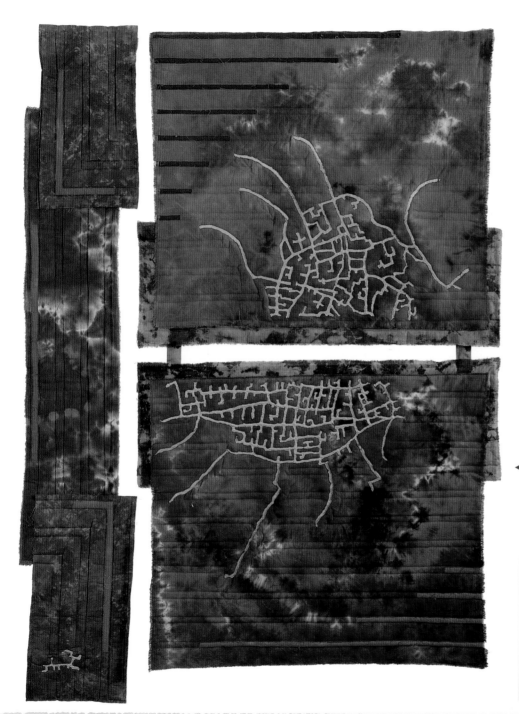

" Unlike the archaeologist, who uncovers deeper and deeper layers of time, I superimpose those layers on my quilts. I focus on the process of understanding the course of time through the assumed meaning of its signs, considering these reminiscences part of our common, ancient knowledge. "

◀ **Break Up** | 2002

56 x 42 inches (1.4 x 1.1 m)
Cotton, hot-cut synthetics; dyed,
negative appliquéd, machine quilted
Photos by Tihanyi-Bakos

Pauline Burbidge

A QUILT-BLOCK FORMAT IMPLIES REPETITION, but in Pauline Burbidge's work the role of repetition undergoes a fascinating metamorphosis. While her early geometric pieced work was based on formal repetition, albeit in very complex ways, in her later work, the blocks are more akin to storyboards, where each repetition signals a change. In Burbidge's Reflections series, her fascination with water reflections led her to use blocks to show how the images on water move, disperse, and reform again. In her pieces that use laminated squares to encapsulate natural items such as feathers or pressed flowers, the repetition actually accentuates the natural variations. Burbidge says this change in how she works has been her response to a desire to create more freely and to bring the process closer to her heart. In basing her designs on her own photographs and collected items, the British artist's work reflects her passion for the countryside of the Scottish Borders, where she lives.

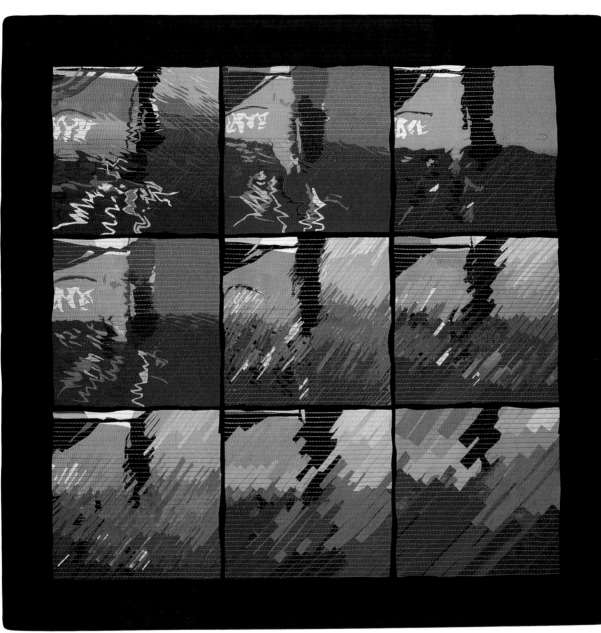

▲ **Pittenweem Quilt** | 2002

59 x 59 inches (1.5 x 1.5 m)
Fabric; collaged, stitched, quilted
Photos by Keith Tidball

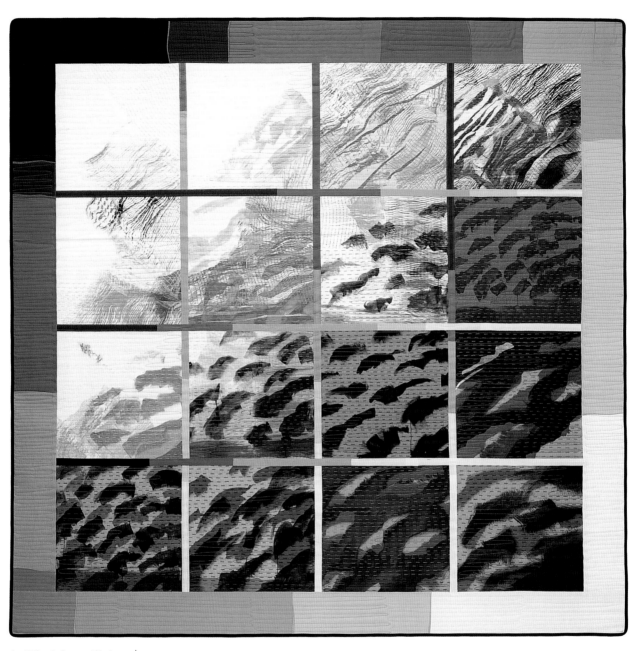

▲ **Wind Over Water** | 2003

77 x 77 inches (2 x 2 m)
Fine cottons and silks; painted, stitched, quilted
Photo by Keith Tidball

▲ Feather Collection II │ 2003

83 x 83 inches (2.1 x 2.1 m)

Cotton, silks, feathers, paint; hand stitched and quilted, painted

Photo by Keith Tidball

" I have always found examples of old quilts to be very inspirational and enjoyed the pure and straightforward use of fabric that quilt making demanded. I have happily linked this with my love of drawing, stitching, and using color. "

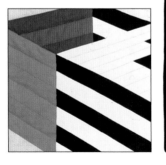

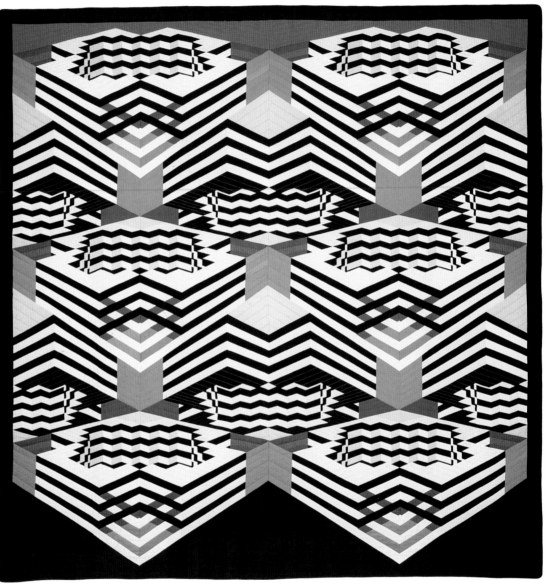

▲ Mirrored Steps | 1983

83 x 79 inches (2.1 x 2 m)

Cotton fabrics; pieced, machine quilted, sink stitched into seams

Photos by John Coles

▲ **Striped Canopy** | 1990

　　96 x 121 inches (2.4 x 3.1 m)
　　Cotton fabrics; pieced, collaged, machine
　　quilted using an industrial quilting machine
　　Photos by Keith Tidball

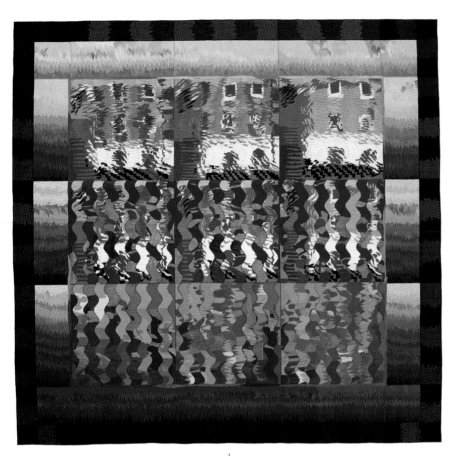

▲ Nottingham Reflections | 1994

   82 x 82 inches (2.1 x 2.1 m)
   Cotton fabrics; collaged, stitched, quilted

   Photos by Keith Tidball

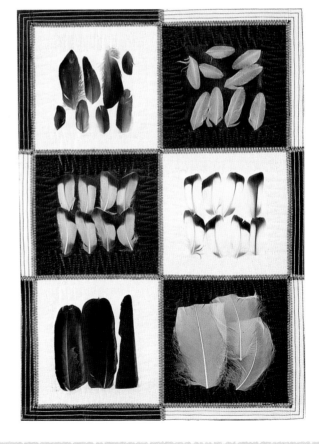

Black and White Feathers | 1996 ▶

   21 x 15 inches (53.3 x 38.1 cm)
   Feathers, fabric; collaged, laminated, stitched

   Photo by Keith Tidball

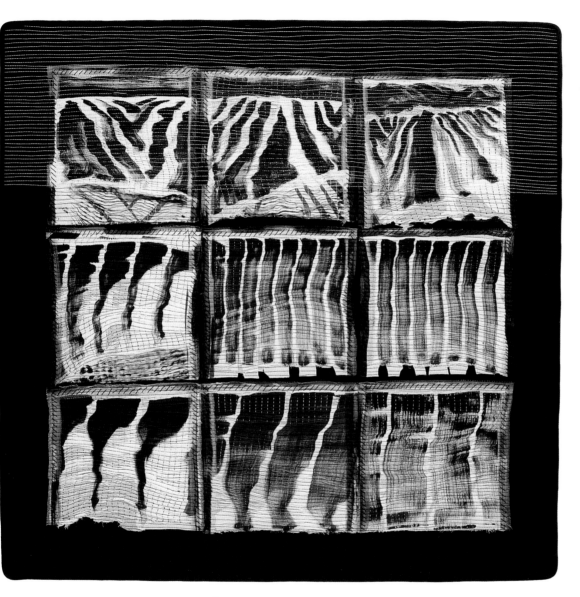

" Learning to dye my own fabric for quilt making opened up possibilities for any color that I chose to dream up. My current use of transparent fabrics, texture, pleating and ruching, and fabric painting all hold exciting possibilities for new work. "

▲ **Climbing the Waterfall** | 2003

38 x 38 inches (96.5 x 96.5 cm)

Fine cotton fabrics; collaged, painted, stitched, quilted

Photos by Keith Tidball

▲ Dancing Lines | 1998

80 x 80 inches (2 x 2 m)
Fabric; collaged, stitched, quilted
Photo by Keith Tidball

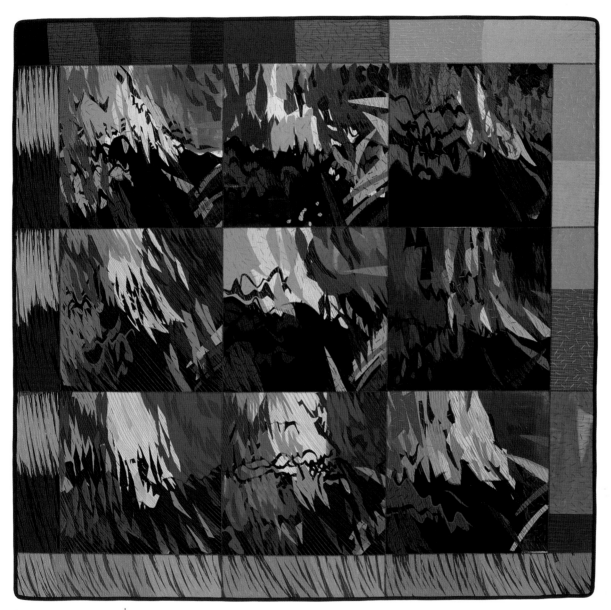

" Using fabric and
stitching to express
myself has always
been a very natural
thing. I feel a work is
most successful when
the image merges
and fuses with the
textile and stitching,
achieving a piece that
could not be made in
anything other than
fabric. "

▲ Paxton Study I | 1997

50 x 50 inches (1.3 x 1.3 m)
Cotton fabrics; collaged, stitched, quilted
Photo by Keith Tidball

Yvonne Porcella

WHEN I THINK OF YVONNE PORCELLA'S QUILTS, I think of red. A beautiful, true red dominates much of her work, accompanied by other vivid crayon-like colors and bordered by graphically bold checkerboard patterns. Several symbols recur throughout her work: the calla lily (a symbol of Porcella's childhood), stars, fish, and chili peppers. One of her most unusual icons is Arnold, a paper doll-type figure, who symbolizes Porcella's relocation to the town of Arnold, California—a move she made after her children had grown up. Another recurring image is a purple Mexican dog of wood and paint depicted in a stylized manner. Each of Porcella's pieces overflows with vibrant color and energy, much like Porcella herself. She founded Studio Art Quilt Associates (SAQA) in 1989 as a membership organization for artists using the quilt as their medium. She served as president of the organization for 11 years. With more than 1,700 members, SAQA is a testament to Porcella's vision and dedication.

▲ Biscuits, Triscuits, and Bones | 1997

41½ x 62 inches (1.1 x 1.6 m)

Cottons; hand appliquéd and quilted, hand pieced

Photos by Sharon Risedorph

▲ **Arnold Meets the Purple Dog** | 1995

46 x 64 inches (1.2 x 1.6 m)
Cottons; hand appliquéd and quilted,
machine pieced

Photo by Sharon Risedorph

" My early focus was based on color alone. My work was created by selecting and arranging fabrics according to what was pleasing. My approach did not include following specific principles of art, such as light to dark value. Rather, my eye simply dictated fabric and color selections. "

▲ Waiting For Pink Linoleum | 2001

   60 x 60 inches (1.5 x 1.5 cm)
   Cottons, silk; hand appliquéd and quilted, machine pieced

   Photo by Sharon Risedorph

**Keep Both Feet
on the Floor** | 1990 ▶

77 x 54 inches (2 x 1.4 m)
Cottons, buttons; patch-
worked, hand appliquéd
and quilted

Photos by Sharon Risedorph

▲ **Come Again Kabuki** | 2004

89 x 76 inches (2.3 x 1.9 m)
Silks, cottons, fabric paint; fused,
machine appliquéd and quilted
Photo by Sharon Risedorph

◀ **Snow on Mt. Fuji** | 1985

132 x 84 inches (3.4 x 2.1 m)
Cottons, silk, poly batting, hand-painted
fabrics; patchworked, pieced
Photo by Sharon Risedorph

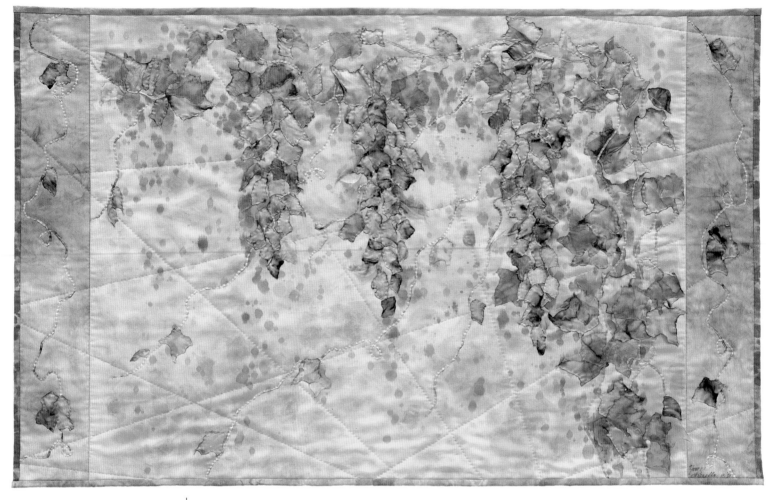

▲ **On Dwight Way** │ 1995

  36 x 53 inches (91.4 x 134.6 cm)
  Silks; burned, appliquéd, hand-painted

  Photos by Sharon Risedorph

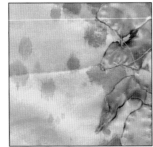

" I like to tell pictorial stories of certain events of time and place. In my years as a weaver and maker of tapestries, I learned to shape colors to form landscapes. Laying in pieces of cotton or silk fabric to create a shape fills my artistic soul. "

◄ **Wisteria le Deuxième** | 1995
42 x 36 inches (106.7 x 91.4 cm)
Silks; hand-painted, burned, appliquéd
Photos by Sharon Risedorph

YVONNE PORCELLA

" American contemporary iconography piqued my interest in the pop-culture images we see in advertising and contemporary art. A series of my quilts using appliqué images of hearts, flowers, dogs, and toys, surrounded by pieced strips of fabric, allowed me to experiment with specific themes that make me smile. "

▲ **America's Hit Parade** | 1999

70½ x 65¼ inches (1.8 x 1.7 m)

Cottons, plywood, beads, glitter, plastic; hand appliquéd, machine appliquéd and pieced

Photo by Sharon Risedorph

▲ Artistic Vision, Man of Vision | 2006

36 x 38 inches (91.4 x 96.5 cm)
Cottons, silks; fused, machine appliquéd and quilted

Photos by David Lutz

M. Joan Lintault

THE IDEA THAT WE LIVE IN PARADISE is what inspires much of M. Joan Lintault's work. The rich surface of her pieces is created from plain white fabric. Because Lintault believes that every process should contribute something to the work, she dyes, overdyes, screenprints, machine embroiders, and paints each image separately, then laboriously stuffs and sews them to

each other or onto a background of her own machine-made lace. The three-dimensional quality of her work is created by shadows that are both painted and created by the lacy interstices of her work. This intensity of working is as important to her as the imagery she uses. Inspired by European paintings of still lifes, which are rich with symbolism but also represent fragments of time and specific objects, Lintault works to create a similar sense of history in her images.

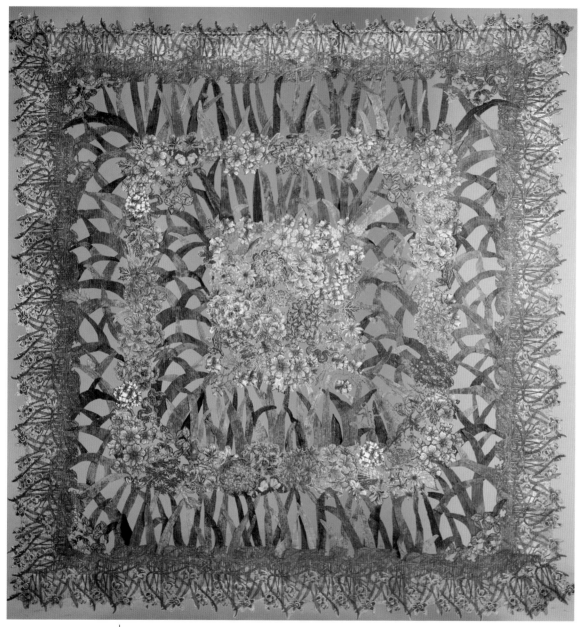

▲ **In the Grass** | 1992

99½ x 93½ inches (2.5 x 2.4 m)

Cotton, sewing machine lace, beads; hand dyed and painted, screen-printed, appliquéd, quilted

Photos by Chris Maitzen

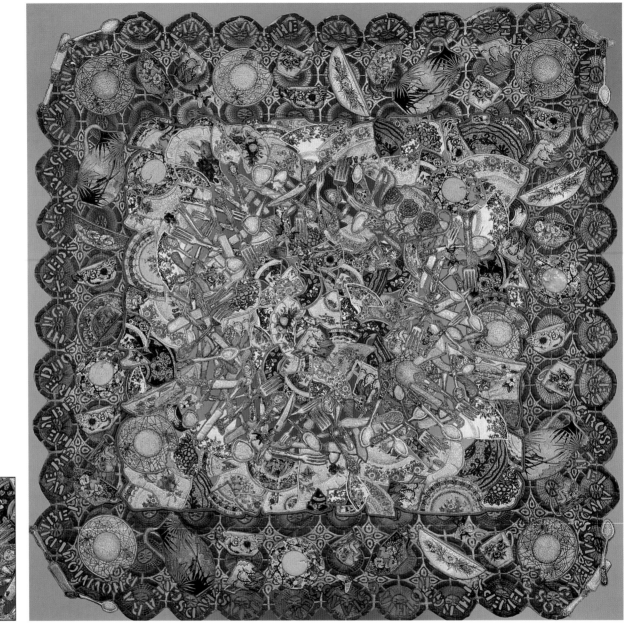

▲ **The Midden** | 2005

58 x 56 inches (1.5 x 1.4 m)

Cotton, sewing machine lace; hand dyed and painted, screen-printed, appliquéd, quilted

Photos by Bob Barrett

▲ **When the Bee Stings** | 1996

95 x 87 inches (2.4 x 2.2 m)

Cotton, sewing machine lace; hand dyed and painted, screen-printed, appliquéd, quilted

Photo by Dan Overturf

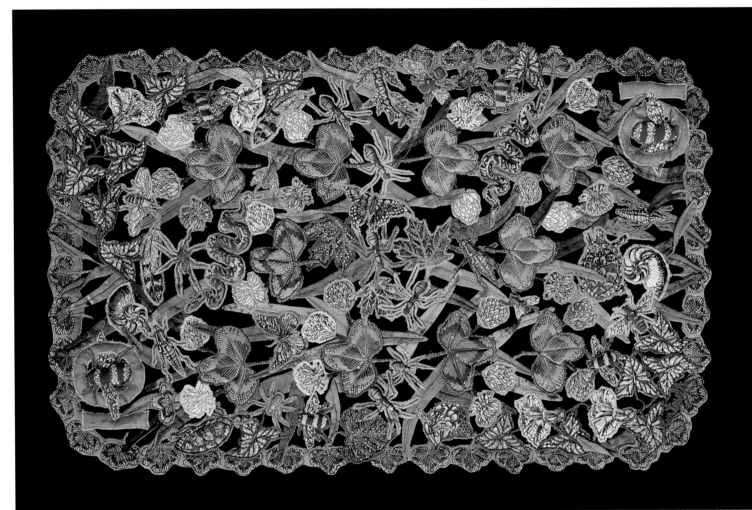

▲ **10 of Clubs** | 1994

18 x 24 inches (45.7 x 61 cm)
Cotton, sewing machine lace, beads;
hand dyed and painted, screen-
printed, appliquéd, quilted

Photo by Breger and Associates

" My work begins with an image, and perhaps a sentence, and then blank white fabric. I love the process of printing and hand coloring because I feel as if I am using a coloring book, something I loved to do when I was younger. "

▲ **Corn Maidens** | 2003

52 x 72 inches (1.3 x 1.8 m)
Cotton, sewing machine lace; hand dyed and
painted, screen-printed, appliquéd, quilted

Photos by Bob Barrett

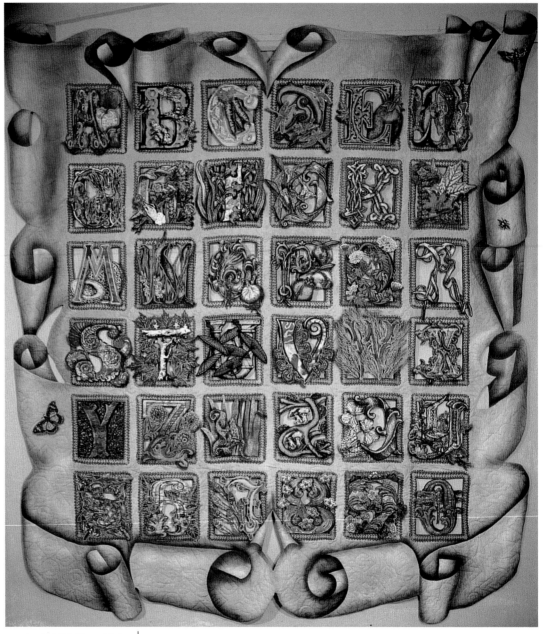

▲ A Riddling Tale │ 1998

97 x 86 inches (2.5 x 2.2 m)
Cotton, sewing machine lace, beads; hand dyed and painted, screen-printed, appliquéd, quilted
Photos by Dan Overturf

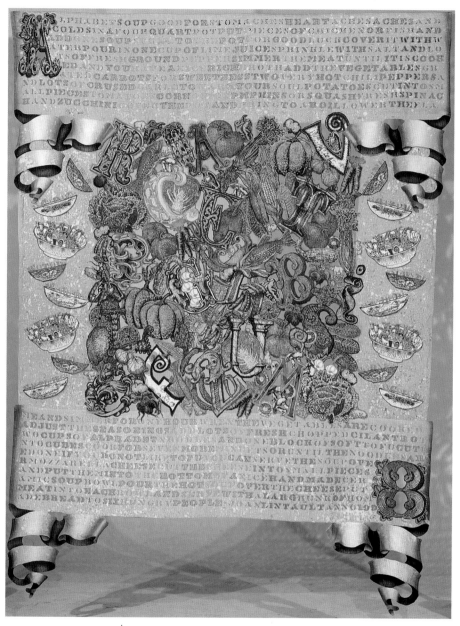

> " My objective is to produce a series of nontraditional quilts that are motivated by metaphors and the evocative use of subject matter. I use the themes of paradise and portraits. The subjects I wish to address are largely traditional and symbolic, such as trees, gardens, flowers, insects, animals, fruit, vegetables, and various objects. "

▲ **Alphabet Soup** | 1998
98 x 74 inches (2.5 x 1.9 m)
Cotton, sewing machine lace; hand dyed and painted,
screen-printed, airbrushed, appliquéd
Photos by Dan Overturf

" I talk about my work in formalist terms because my work is first and foremost about the visual and formal elements of art: line, shape, color, form, negative space, and positive shape, and how these elements function on the picture plane I've created. I think these elements are what makes art powerful. "

▲ Fan Dancer | 2004
59 x 56 inches (149.9 x 142.2 cm)
Cotton, machine-made lace; hand dyed, screen-printed, painted, appliquéd, quilted, machine embroidered
Photos by Bob Barrett

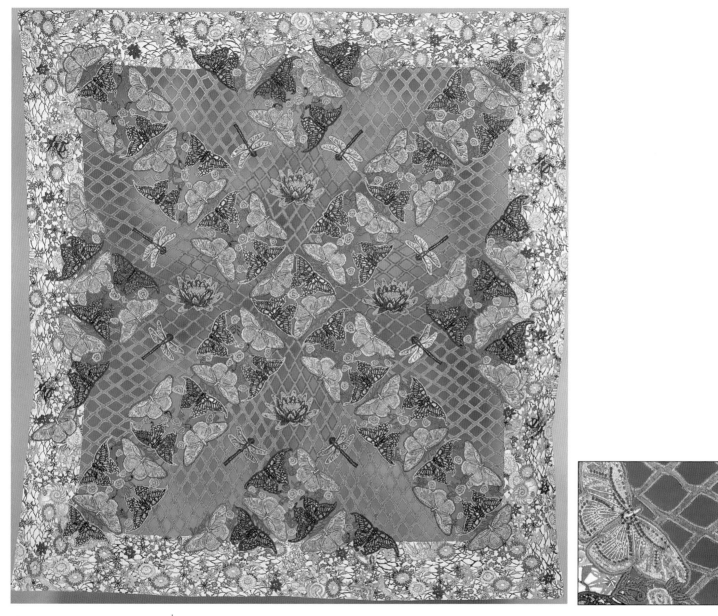

▲ **Times of the Butterfly** | 2003

68¼ x 65½ inches (1.7 x 1.7 m)
Cotton, rice paper resist, sewing machine lace; hand dyed and painted,
screen-printed and stenciled, appliquéd, quilted, machine embroidered
Photos by Bob Barrett

Katie Pasquini Masopust

A CONSTANT CREATIVE RESTLESSNESS is indicative of the dynamic energy Katie Pasquini Masopust brings to everything she does. Her style has gone through many different phases, each accompanied by the publication of a book and a busy teaching schedule, as she shared her new passion with other quilters. Her first book was about mandala designs. Then she explored three-dimensional illusions, which branched into isometric perspective pieces. She then switched to exploring landscapes based on her photography, adding to them through the illusion of color transparencies and ghost layers. Recently, her work has returned to the abstract and is based on her paintings. The early work in this new series translated her painting into fabric. For her more current pieces, Pasquini Masopust cuts up these painted canvases and reassembles them into new work. A longtime leader in the field of art quilting, Pasquini Masopust was the president of Studio Art Quilt Associates from 2000 to 2007 and was awarded the Silver Star for lifetime achievement in quilting at the International Quilt Festival in 2005.

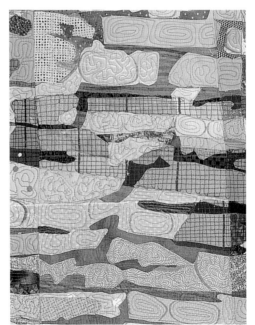

◄ **Passages Chaco** | 1997

60 x 45 inches (1.5 x 1.1 m)
Cottons and blends, lamé, satin,
wool batting; machine appliquéd,
pieced and quilted

Photos by Hawthorne Studio

▲ **Staccato** | 2006

44 x 60 inches (1.1 x 1.5 m)

Cottons and blends; machine appliquéd and quilted

Photo by Carolyn Wright

▲ **Leggiero** | 2005

80 x 80 inches (2 x 2 m)

Cottons and blends; machine appliquéd and quilted

Photo by Carolyn Wright

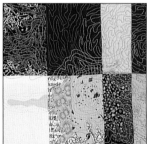

▲ **Black & White Getty** | 1998

45 x 60 inches (1.1 x 1.5 m)
Cottons and blends, lamé, satin,
wool batting; machine appliquéd,
pieced and quilted

Photos by Hawthorne Studio

Dimensional Portal | 1994 ▶

83 x 83 inches (2.1 x 2.1 m)
Cottons and blends; machine pieced,
hand appliquéd and quilted

Photo by Lindsay Olsen

" I begin my work with the camera. I take several shots of my subject, looking for a strong composition. I create drawings from the photographs, changing each as I go. I then determine if the composition is as I intend. If necessary, I make another drawing, changing it for the final time before having it enlarged as a full-size pattern. "

◀ **Painted Canyon** | 2004
90 x 54 inches (2.3 x 1.4 m)
Cottons and blends; machine appliquéd and quilted
Photos by Hawthorne Studio

▲ Stairs | 2001

65 x 60 inches (1.7 x 1.5 m)

Cottons and blends; machine appliquéd and quilted

Photo by Hawthorne Studio

▲ Rio Hondo | 1994

54 x 80 inches (1.4 x 2 m)
Cottons and blends, lamé, satin, wool batting;
machine appliquéd, pieced and quilted

Photos by Hawthorne Studio

▲ **Musical View** | 2006

    37 x 40 inches (94 x 101.6 cm)

    Canvas, acrylic paint; painted, machine quilted

    Photo by Carolyn Wright

" Lately, I have returned
to my painting roots
and have been creating
quilts directly from my
paintings. In my latest
work, I have used acrylic
paints to create my
images on treated canvas.
I then cut the canvas,
reassemble, and machine
stitch to add dimension. "

▲ **Summer Nights** | 2006

52 x 39 inches (132.1 x 99.1 cm)

Canvas, acrylic paint; painted, machine quilted

Photos by Carolyn Wright

Nancy N. Erickson

A SENSE OF LONELINESS pervades the works of Nancy N. Erickson. Her large quilted whole-cloth paintings of polar bears, cougars, capybaras, wolves, and spirit guides are commentaries on the loss of connection between humans and the animals with which we share the planet. While the works often contain humor, they all seem to emphasize the separateness of the beings they depict. Early works placed groups of animals in man-made settings, struggling to come to terms with an imagined post-nuclear period. Erickson's sense of humor is often reflected in juxtapositions, such as cougars watching television or polar bears painting paw prints on the walls of a cave. In recent work the animals more often are alone, their bodies forming the entire work and encompassing a variety of markings resembling cave paintings. While the markings painted on the animal figures may contain groups of animals, the overall figure is solitary, an elegiac commentary on loss of home and community.

Pleistocene Memory │ 2005 ▶

78 x 74 inches (2 x 1.9 m)
Velvet, fabric paints, charcoal,
satin; painted, machine stitched
and appliquéd, cut

Photos by artist

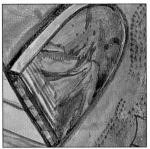

◀ **Hall of Memory #7: The Wondrous Green Room** | 1998

59¾ x 59 inches (1.5 x 1.5 m)
Fabric, sparkle and pearlescent paints; painted,
machine stitched, appliquéd and quilted

Photos by artist

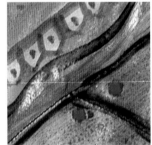

◀ **CONFINED** | 1995

57 x 59 inches (1.5 x 1.5 m)
Pearlescent paints; painted,
machine stitched and appliquéd

Photos by artist

▲ It's Not All That Easy Getting Everyone into the Group Portrait | 1996

48½ x 69¾ inches (1.2 x 1.8 m)

Fabric and pearlescent paints; painted, machine stitched and appliquéd

Photo by artist

▲ **The Clear and Present Danger** | 1987

86 x 77 inches (2.2 x 2 m)
Satin, velvet, cotton; painted, appliquéd,
machine stitched

Photo by artist

▲ **The Black Wolf** | 2006

   68 x 65 inches (1.7 x 1.7 m)
   Whole cloth, velvet, satin; shaped, appliquéd,
   painted, machine and hand stitched
   Photo by Brian Blauser

"All the works shown here are part of an ongoing series of visual narratives taking place in a post-nuclear time in an artist's studio. These works attempt to respond to the loneliness we all experience and to indicate possibilities for the future with all of us together. "

▲ **Retelling Orion** | 1988

    55 x 71 inches (1.4 x 1.8 m)
    Satin, cottons; painted, sewn
    Photo by artist

" All of the quilts point to the importance of community in a future time and to an acknowledgment of the bears, ravens, lions, cougars, and wolves as powerful elements in life. These individuals act as familiars, or spiritual guides in the lives of humans, and it is they who reestablish communities and retell the old myths. "

▲ **Felis Forever (1)** | 2000

39 x 69 inches (99.1 x 175.3 cm)
Velvet, fabric paints; painted,
machine stitched, appliquéd
and quilted

Photos by artist

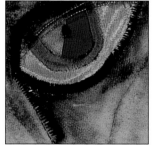

▲ **The Visitation** | 1984

72 x 84 inches (1.8 x 2.1 m)

Satin, velvet, cotton; painted, appliquéd, machine stitched

Photo by artist

" The commonly accepted name now is art quilts, but for a while I called my pieces 'quilteds' to emphasize my methods. These works are painted and stitched as quilts, added to and backed as quilts, but they are really 'quilteds,' or layered, stitched paintings. "

◀ **Interiors #5: The Cat's Story** | 1985
117 x 56 inches (3 x 1.4 m)
Satin, velvet, cotton; painted,
appliquéd, machine stitched
Photos by artist

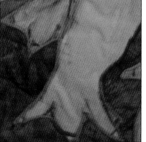

Susan Shie

COOKING IS VERY IMPORTANT TO SUSAN SHIE, both in her daily life and in her work. Gardens, her family, pincushions, cats, and the tarot also are frequent iconic images in Shie's painted, airbrushed, and embellished diary quilt paintings. Shie's early works were heavily quilted and embellished, often in collaboration with her husband, James Acord. Her recent works depend much more on the almost hypergraphic writing that covers the surface of each piece, as Shie diaries the events in her life that occur during the time she is creating the quilt. Especially since a switch to using an airbrush pen, Shie's writing has a lyric quality, flowing around the images of her painted backgrounds. Her increased use of writing as a decorative element has led her to gradually eliminate the heavy embellishment typical of earlier work. But while the techniques may have altered, the sense of an artist who has always had to "work recklessly...tell[ing] stories of daily life" remains unchanged.

◀ **The Teapot/High Priestess:
Card #2 in the Kitchen Tarot** | 1998

In collaboration with James Acord

87 x 55 inches (2.2 x 1.4 m)
Fabric, fabric paint, jewelry, beads, wood,
buttons, Indian handbags, lace, leather;
painted, hand sewn, embroidered and
tooled, airbrushed, appliquéd

Photos by Brian Blauser

▲ **Rainbow Garden** | 1996

In collaboration with James Acord

78 x 94 inches (2 x 2.4 m)

Cotton, figures, forms, wooden spoons, tomato pin cushions, fabric basket, bottle caps, found doll, clothespins, wood; quilted, hand and airbrush painted, written, cut, hand sewn and tooled, embroidered

Photos by Brian Blauser

▲ Katrina Blues | 2005

45 x 75 inches (1.1 x 1.9 m)
Cotton, beads; drawn and written,
whole-cloth brush painted, machine
crazy-grid quilted

Photos by artist

" I am a painter and storyteller, and I use my art quilts to communicate. I tell stories of life around me and mix in my own social and political commentary, working with whatever is on my mind at the time and mixing things together in unexpected ways. "

Year of the Dog | 2006 ▶

68 x 45 inches (1.7 x 1.1 m)
Cotton, beads; drawn and written, whole-cloth brush painted,
machine crazy-grid quilted

Photos by artist

" Since 1998, I've been working on my *Kitchen Tarot* project, in which I choose a kitchen object for each traditional card's quilt. The kitchen is my 'deck,' because I use cooking as a metaphor for the goodness and holistic presence we need to nurture in the world. "

◀ **The Punch Bowl/Star: Card #17 in the Kitchen Tarot** | 2006

84 x 63 inches (2.1 x 1.6 m)
Whole-cloth cotton, paint, beads; painted, written, machine crazy-grid quilted

Photos by artist

◀ **The Lost and Found** | 1988

102 x 96 inches (2.6 x 2.4 m)
Cotton, fabric paint, silk, figures,
beads, found objects; brush painted,
hand stuffed, embroidered and sewn

Photos by artist

Tropical New York | 1988 ▶

90 x 90 inches (2.3 x 2.3 m)
Cotton, acrylic paint, beads, polymer clay, crystals, found objects,
mussel shells; hand brushed,
quilted and embroidered

Photos by Brian Blauser

▲ **The World of the Wonderous** │ 1991

In collaboration with James Acord

75 x 72 inches (1.9 x 1.8 m)

Brush and fabric paint, beads, fabric plant thorns by Lisa Kane, padded figures, masks, brass shields, leather; hand quilted, embroidered, beaded, painted, tooled, sewn and stitched

Main photo by Stewart Simonds; detail by artist

SUSAN SHIE

" Learning to use an airbrush pen helped me shift from obsessive hand-work to simple machine grid sewing, because I no longer had to hand-embroider over my writing and drawings to achieve rich, crisp lines. I decided to leave embellishment out of my work and allow the detailed painting and writing to stand alone. "

▲ **Prayer for Oklahoma City** | 1996

In collaboration with James Acord

86 x 78 inches (2.2 x 2 m)

Whole-cloth cotton, beads, buttons, fabric paint; hand and airbrush painted, hand and machine sewn

Photos by artist

▲ **Year of the Monkey** | 1992

In collaboration with James Acord
62 x 55 inches (1.6 x 1.4 m)
Fabric paint, cotton, masks, leather, polymer clay hands; hand
painted, embroidered and tooled, machine and hand stitched

Photos by Brian Blauser

Caryl Bryer Fallert

EXACTING PRECISION AND ORGANIC FORM may seem an unlikely pair of descriptive phrases, but they both fit the work of Caryl Bryer Fallert. My first introduction to Fallert's work was seeing one of her twisted tucks pieces displayed at a local quilt show. I was mesmerized and spent more than half an hour just walking from one side of the piece to the other, watching how it changed as I moved. Fallert calls the works in this series "viewer participation art." The piece I saw is one of more than 150 pieces exploring variations of this theme. Fallert's later work is characterized by the inclusion of her hand-dyed fabrics in a color-saturated, full spectrum to create a sense of sheer exuberance and joy. Birds soar in flight surrounded by whirling ribbons of shapes. Brilliant colors fill the entire field of view, and swirls of quilting give texture to the designs. Fallert says of her quilts, "It is my hope they will lift the spirits and delight the eyes of those who see them," and she truly succeeds.

▲ Flying Free #2 | 1995

93 x 82 inches (2.4 x 2.1 m)
Cotton; hand dyed and painted, machine pieced and quilted

Photos by artist

FALLERT

▲ **Birds of a Different Color** | 1999

93 x 74 inches (2.4 x 1.9 m)
Cotton, batting; hand dyed and painted, machine pieced and quilted

Photos by artist

▲ **Feather Study #10** | 1999

48 x 48 inches (1.2 x 1.2 m)
Cotton, batting; hand dyed and painted,
machine pieced and quilted

Photos by artist

◀ **Dancing with the Shadow #1: Harmony** | 1995

> 63 x 93 inches (1.6 x 2.4 m)
> Cotton, batting; hand dyed and painted, machine pieced, appliquéd and quilted
>
> Photo by artist

Checking Over the ▶ Rainbow #17 | 1994

> 46½ x 77 inches (1.2 x 2 m)
> Cotton, wool batting; hand dyed and painted, machine pieced, pleated and quilted
>
> Photo by artist

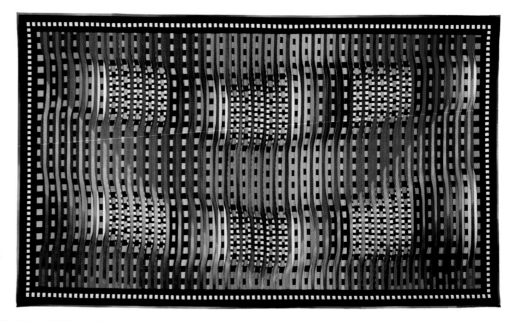

" The focus of my work
is on the qualities of
color, line, and texture,
which engage the spirit
and emotions of the
viewer, evoking a sense
of mystery, excitement,
or joy. Illusions of
movement, depth, and
luminosity are common to
most of my work. "

◀ **Messenger #2** | 1996
67 x 51 inches (1.7 x 1.3 m)
Cotton, batting; hand
painted, machine
appliquéd and quilted
Photo by artist

◀ **Spirogyra** | 2002

65 x 44 inches (1.7 x 1.1 m)
Cotton, batting; hand dyed and painted,
machine pieced, appliquéd and quilted
Photos by artist

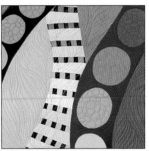

❝ Most of my current work is made
from cotton fabric, which is first
hand dyed and painted, then
pieced, appliquéd, embroidered,
and quilted by machine. Textures
created by layering, pleating,
and quilting invite the viewer to
touch as well as look. ❞

▲ Midnight Fantasy #1 | 1999

48 x 48 inches (1.2 x 1.2 m)

Cotton, batting; hand dyed and painted, machine pieced and quilted

Photo by artist

▲ Farewell to the Silver Bird | 1997

48 x 48 inches (1.2 x 1.2 m)

Cotton, nylon, batting; hand dyed and painted, machine pieced, appliquéd and quilted

Photo by artist

" After many years of painting, sewing, and experimenting with other media, I discovered that fabric, as an artistic medium, best expressed my personal vision. I love the tactile qualities of cloth and the unlimited color range made possible by hand dyeing and painting. "

◀ New Dawn | 2000

90 x 72 inches
(2.3 x 1.8 m)
Cotton, various synthetic
fibers, batting; hand dyed
and painted, machine
pieced, appliquéd and
quilted

Photos by artist

CARYL BRYER FALLERT

Jeanette Gilks

A PAINTING AND DRAWING TEACHER, South African Jeanette Gilks says much of her work is "woven from African elements." While she does not mean her pieces are literally woven, her use of strips of color and fringe creates a strong visual reference to more traditional woven fibers. African animals, birds, bugs, and fish populate much of Gilks' work. Other works are completely abstract. Some pieces explore color juxtapositions, some express political ideas, and others reflect her reactions to the landscape around her.

The striations of color that form the backgrounds of her work are most often in the golden sand tones of the bush. Other works are lush in their use of blues, greens, and purples. Art quilts are often defined as art created by using fabric as one's palette. In Gilks' work, the painting metaphor is even more apt than usual: Her works look like they were painted using strips of cloth instead of stripes of paint.

▲ **Free Fall** | 2004

49 x 49 inches (1.2 x 1.2 m)
Commercial cottons, upholstery materials; layered, machine
stitched and embroidered, appliquéd, reverse appliquéd

Photos by Stephanie Stein

▲ **Ode to Joy** | 1991

19½ x 25½ inches (49.5 x 64.8 cm)
Commercially printed fabrics, net, fabric
stabilizer; manipulated, layered, fused

Photo by artist

" I enjoy the tactile immediacy of fibers and textiles and the rich

associations their ready-made qualities bring to an artwork.

Like sculpture, textile art conveys a powerful, physical sense of

presence—a *hereness* as opposed to a *thereness*. "

◄ **Windows for All Seasons** | 1992

52 x 40 inches (1.3 x 1 m)
Commercial cotton
fabrics; ripped, frayed,
machine sewn, hand
quilted, appliquéd and
reverse appliquéd

Photos by artist

▲ Hunting Season | 1996

53 x 48 inches (1.4 x 1.2 m)
Commercial cottons, upholstery fabrics, wool, animal fur, leather, fish hooks, bullet cartridges, animal bones; appliquéd, reverse appliquéd, machine stitched, free-motion machine embroidered

Photo by artist

▲ **Mirage** │ 1995

45½ x 58½ inches (1.2 x 1.5 m)

Commercial cottons, voile, metallic and upholstery fabrics; ripped, frayed, appliquéd, reverse appliquéd, machine sewn, free-motion machine embroidered, drawn with a needle

Photos by artist

237

" I was brought up in Africa—a continent rich in textile traditions. The particular spirit of a fabric or a technique can contribute significantly to the meaning of an artwork. "

▲ **Screens—Major Minor Signatures** | 2004

12 x 47 x 4 inches (30.5 x 119.4 x 10.2 cm)
Card, paper, fabric stabilizer, cotton;
photocopied, collaged, machine sewn

Photos by Ian Carbutt

▲ Hear Rings │ 1999

25 x 25 inches (63.5 x 63.5 cm)
Fabric stabilizer, paper, cotton; collaged, sewn, machine stitched
Photo by artist

Jane Burch Cochran

GLOVES MAY BE what Jane Burch Cochran is best known for. Gloves appear in almost every piece she makes. For her, they represent hands "reaching and searching for questions about...the human psyche," and they also perform more prosaic functions—holding things or reaching into pockets. And sometimes they become angel wings. Blackbirds, dresses, moons, and hidden pockets are other recurring images in her work. Heavily embellished with found objects, beads, buttons, yo-yos, and paint, Cochran's work develops intuitively as she adds layer upon layer of appliqué and embellishment to her free-form, strip-pieced patchwork base. Cochran describes herself as part moon chaser, part gypsy butterfly, and part pearly queen (after the Cockney costumes covered in buttons). Her recent work explores our complex relationships with food, while a new series is inspired by her trips to Mexico for Día de los Muertos.

◄ Moonlight | 2007

77 x 61 inches (2 x 1.6 m)
Various fabrics, beads,
buttons, paint, glove,
doilies, embroidery thread;
machine pieced and appli-
quéd, hand appliquéd and
quilted

Photos by Pam Monfort

" In my art quilts, I try to combine my training in painting, my love of fabric, and the tradition of American quilting. I unconsciously combine the loose, free feeling of abstract painting with the time-consuming and controlled techniques of sewing and beading. "

▲ **Looking for God** | 1996

74 x 64 inches (1.9 x 1.6 m)
Various fabrics, beads, buttons, paint, gloves, sequins, chalk, cloth leaves, child's dress, pot holder, embroidery thread; machine pieced, stamped, hand appliquéd and quilted, beaded
Photos by Pam Monfort

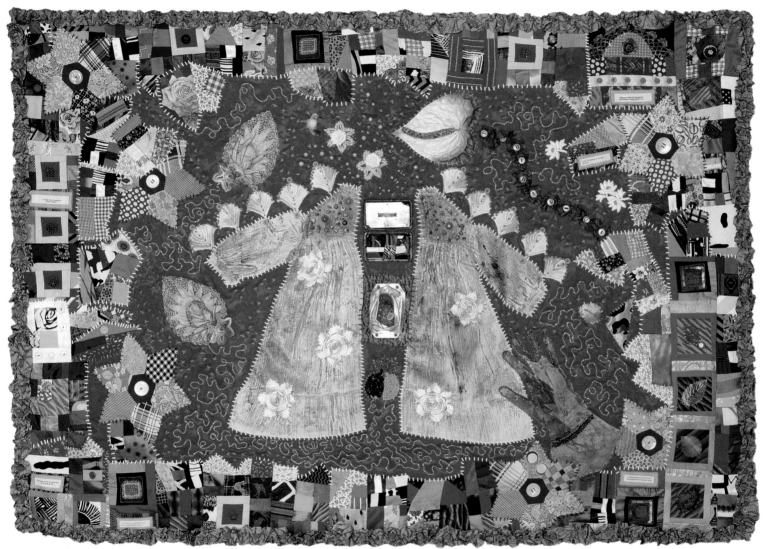

▲ A Quilt for the Child I Never Had | 1998

  39 x 55 inches (99.1 x 139.7 cm)
  Various fabrics, beads, buttons, etching inks, found clothing
  and objects, paint, photocopied fortunes on fabric, embroidery
  thread; machine pieced, hand appliquéd and quilted

Photos by Pam Monfort

▲ **Winged Victory (c. 1900-2000)** | 1999

68 x 71 inches (1.7 x 1.8 m)

Various fabrics, beads, buttons, paint, found clothing and objects, embroidery thread, acrylic paint; machine pieced, stamped, hand appliquéd, quilted and embellished

Photo by Pam Monfort

" My quilts are considered
narrative because
some of the imagery is
recognizable. The quilt
does not usually tell a
particular story—it's left
to viewers to see and
translate what they will.
My quilts are highly
embellished with beads,
buttons, and paint to
enhance the narrative
with a unique and
personal texture. "

▲ **Deviled and Angel** | 2003

55 x 64 inches (1.4 x 1.6 m)
Various fabrics, beads, buttons, paint, gloves, sequins,
glitter, net, blouse, handkerchief, doily; machine
pieced and quilted, hand appliquéd

Photo by Pam Monfort

JANE BURCH COCHRAN

▲ **Surprise Party** | 1991

72 x 64 inches (1.8 x 1.6 m)
Various fabrics, beads, buttons, paint, gloves, sequins, artificial flowers and leaves, found objects; machine pieced, hand beaded and appliquéd

Photos by Pam Monfort

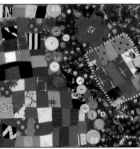

▲ **The Last Dance** | 1990

79 x 69 inches (2 x 1.8 m)
Various fabrics, beads, buttons, sequins, glitter, gloves, dress, fabric flowers, paint, gesso, canvas; machine pieced, hand appliquéd and embellished

Photos by Pam Monfort

▲ **Life Line** | 1994

68 x 82 inches (1.7 x 2.1 m)
Various fabrics, found clothing, beads, buttons, paint, colored pencil, embroidery
thread; machine pieced, appliquéd, hand embellished and quilted

Photo by Pam Monfort

▲ **Paper Plates and Bone China, Some Hand Painted** | 1999

41 x 52 inches (1 x 1.3 m)

Various fabrics, paper, beads, buttons, paint, silver leaf, glove, vintage quilt pieces, ribbon, photocopied fortunes, doily stencil, embroidery thread; machine and hand appliquéd, hand quilted

Photos by Pam Monfort

▲ **Shroud for a Colorful Soul** | 2005

44 x 66 inches (1.1 x 1.7 m)
Various fabrics, beads, buttons, paint,
sequins, gloves, found crocheted items;
machine pieced, hand and machine
appliquéd, hand embellished

Photo by Pam Monfort

" I often use recycled gloves, doilies, potholders, dresses, and

other old fabric pieces to create a new narrative. "

Pamela Allen

WHAT STRIKES YOU FIRST ABOUT PAMELA ALLEN'S ART are the faces. Never mind that they are often blue or green; never mind that the eyes and mouths are on different planes, often executed in different styles, reminding the viewer of Picasso. These faces are compelling. They are expressive. And they demand that you share their emotion. The Canadian artist's fabric-collage narrative works are snapshots that seem to have caught their subjects in particularly revealing moments.

Often humorous and created in Allen's funky-folksy style, each piece features one or two oversized people, heavily embellished with all sorts of miniature items found by this self-described consummate bargain hunter in order to develop the narrative. There are utensils and plastic food for a kitchen table; safety pins and sewing bobbins for a mother; and fish, birds, and bugs for a landscape. And Allen says, "There is always the chance I might add some more stuff if the mood hits me."

◀ **Crone of Crazy** | 2002

53 x 40 inches (1.4 x 1 m)
Recycled and commercial fabrics,
beads, safety pins, plastic eggs
and fruit, stuffed elements; hand
raw-edge appliqué, machine
quilted, embellished

Photos by artist

" I have what most quilters would think of as a pitifully small stash of fabric. I rarely buy yardage, but make most of my images from recycled thrift shop clothing. I like the idea that these fabrics come to me with a hidden life I know nothing about. "

▲ Queen Bee | 2002

58 x 44 inches (1.5 x 1.1 m)
Recycled and commercial fabrics, found and manufactured objects; hand raw-edge appliqué, machine quilted, embellished

Photos by artist

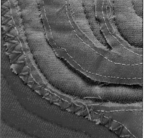

◀ **Lillian Hellman Taking the Oath Before HUAC** | 2002

60 x 45 inches (1.5 x 1.1 m)
Recycled and commercial
fabrics, found and manufactured objects; hand raw-edge
appliqué, machine quilted,
embellished

Photos by artist

▲ **Out of Touch** | 2004

54 x 48 inches (1.4 x 1.2 m)
Recycled and commercial fabrics, found and manufactured objects;
hand raw-edge appliqué, machine quilted, embellished
Photo by artist

▲ Birdbrain | 2002

   57 x 37 inches (144.8 x 94 cm)
   Recycled and commercial fabrics, found
   and manufactured objects; hand raw-edge
   appliqué, machine quilted, embellished
   Photo by artist

▲ Cherry Pickers | 2005

   25 x 20 inches (63.5 x 50.8 cm)
   Recycled and commercial fabrics, found
   and manufactured objects; hand raw-edge
   appliqué, machine quilted, embellished
   Photo by artist

" Narrative, or at the very
least, figurative references
are important in my work.
A piece has to have a
personal meaning for me in
order for it to maintain my
interest. I do tend to create
little scenarios as the work
unfolds, starting with one
idea, which spawns another
and another. "

PAMELA ALLEN

Cold Canadians | 2005 ▶

47 x 33 inches (119.4 x 83.8 cm)
Recycled and commercial fabrics,
found and manufactured objects,
polymer clay, eyelash scarf; hand
raw-edge appliqué, machine
quilted, embellished

Photo by artist

▲ **Woman with a Bird on Her Arm** │ 2006

20 x 20 inches (50.8 x 50.8 cm)
Recycled and commercial fabrics, found and manufactured objects;
hand raw-edge appliqué, machine quilted, embellished
Photo by artist

▲ **One Hot Mama** | 2006

54 x 51 inches (1.4 x 1.3 m)
Recycled and commercial fabrics, found and manufactured objects, polymer
clay, beads; hand raw-edge appliqué, machine quilted, embellished

Photos by artist

" Progress in my work is often determined by the story that is taking shape. The materials, of course, do determine the outcome somewhat, but I think that my thought process—the stream-of-consciousness that is taking place—determines most of my design choices. "

◀ Eve Under Scrutiny II | 2005
37 x 25 inches (94 x 63.5 cm)
Recycled and commercial fabrics, found and manufactured objects; hand raw-edge appliqué, machine quilted, embellished
Photo by artist

Therese May

WHIMSICAL FOLK-ART ANIMALS, bright and cheerful colors, a surface covered with circles and dots of paint? It must be a work by Therese May. An artist for whom more is more, May is inspired by art made by combining countless small pieces of colors and shapes, such as in mosaics, millefiori, or the Watts Towers. Though she bases her designs around bold, simple appliqué shapes, May then often embellishes every bit of the surfaces of her work with beads, buttons, and three-dimensional dots of acrylic paint. Repetition is an important design element in her work, both in her use of a grid structure and in her embellishment patterns, especially of paint dots. Another series of work explores repeating faces divided into myriad pieces created from a scrap bag of unusual fabrics. These repeating human, elf, or animal visages create whimsical delights. May's life-affirming philosophy that art is a path to healing, both for the individual and for the world, shines through in her vibrant, uplifting designs.

▲ **Affirmation Quilt** | 2006

71 x 61 inches (1.8 x 1.6 m)

Fabric, acrylic paint, fabric paint, buttons, jewels; machine appliquéd, machine quilted by Jenny Michael

Photos by Richard Johns

▲ **Birthday Quilt Goddess** | 2003

47 x 47 inches (1.2 x 1.2 m)

Fabric, acrylic paint, jewels; machine appliquéd, machine quilted by Jenny Michael

Photo by Richard Johns

▲ **Mandala Teapot** | 2005

53 x 56 inches (1.4 x 1.4 m)
Fabric; machine appliquéd, machine quilted by Jenny Michael

Photo by Richard Johns

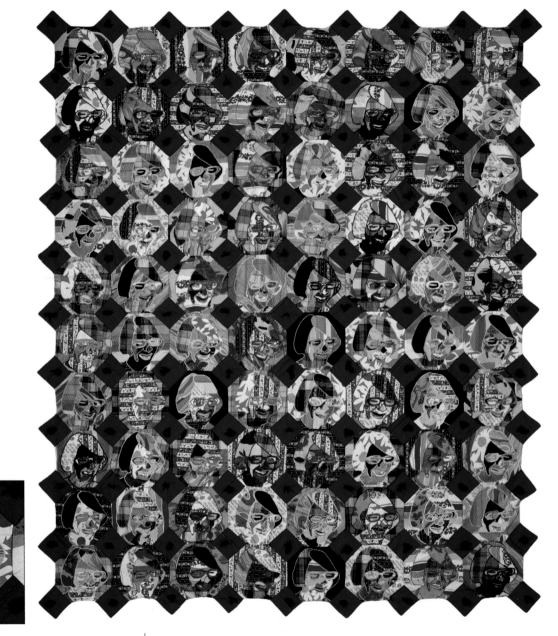

" I love the idea of taking what you already have and creating something new from it. "

▲ **Therese Quilt** | 1969

90 x 72 inches (2.3 x 1.8 m)
Fabric; puzzle interchange, machine appliquéd, hand tied
Photos by artist

▲ **Here Now** | 2007

23 x 31 inches (58.4 x 78.7 cm)
Fabric, acrylic and fabric paint,
buttons, beads, braids, yarn; machine
appliquéd and quilted

Photos by Richard Johns

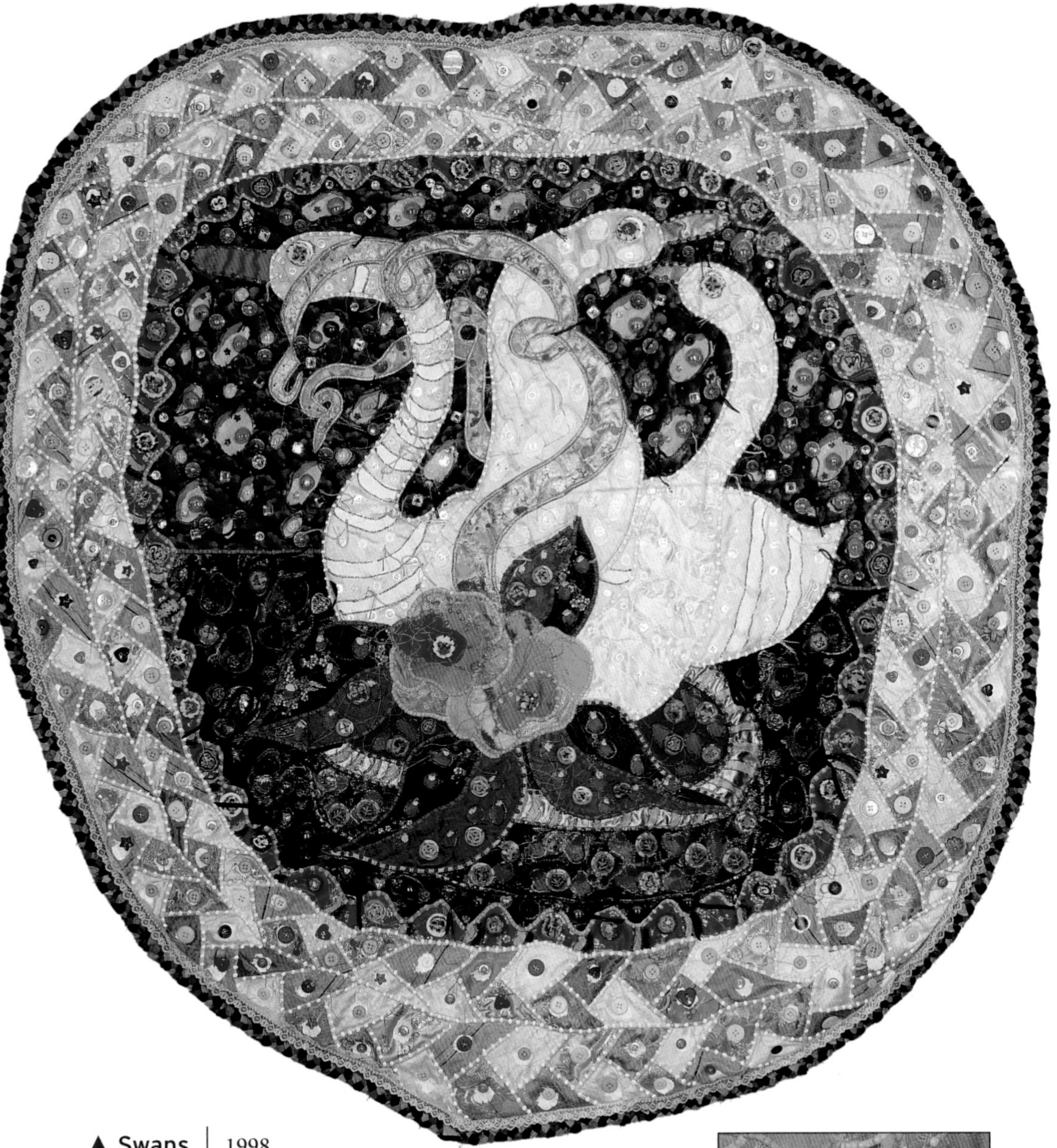

▲ Swans | 1998

50 x 47 inches (1.3 x 1.2 m)
Fabric, acrylic and fabric paint, polymer clay and regular
buttons, braids, lace; machine appliquéd, hand tied

Photos by Richard Johns

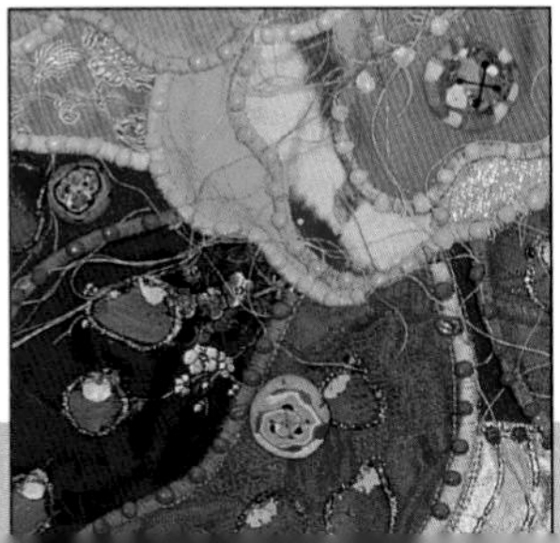

" My art quilts are fabric creations filled with warmth, color, and life-enhancing materials that add vibrancy and optimism to the viewer's environment. In creating these wall hangings, my intention is to visually uplift and energize both the viewer and the space. The concept of hope and inspiration, which I feel is needed at this time, is central to the themes of my work. "

▲ House Flower | 2000

22 x 19 inches (55.9 x 48.3 cm)
Fabric, acrylic and fabric paint, polymer clay and regular buttons,
beads, braids; machine appliquéd, hand embroidered
Photo by Richard Johns

THERESE MAY

▲ I Am Who I Am | 2003

38 x 16 inches (96.5 x 40.6 cm)
Fabric, acrylic and fabric paints,
jewels; puzzle interchange,
machine appliquéd, machine
quilted by Jenny Michael

Photo by Richard Johns

▲ Love House | 2002

78 x 58 inches (2 x 1.5 m)
Fabric, acrylic paint, handmade rubber stamp; machine appliquéd
and embroidered, machine quilted by Jenny Michael

Photo by Richard Johns

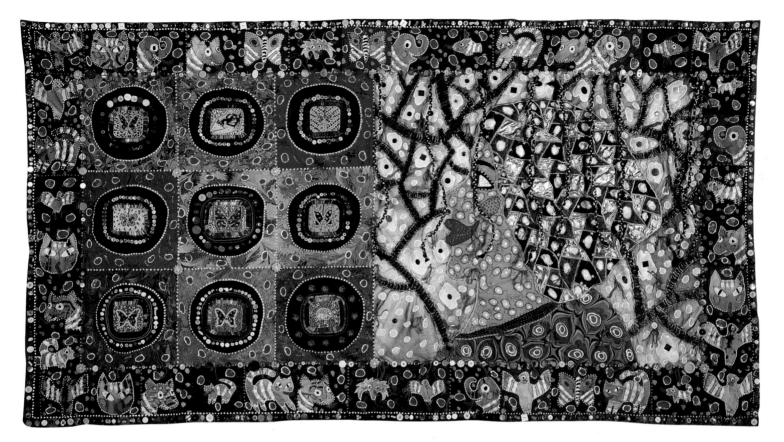

▲ **Contemplating the Ninepatch** | 1994

50 x 92 inches (1.3 x 2.3 m)
Fabric, acrylic and fabric paint, beads, buttons, polymer clay,
braids; machine appliquéd, hand embroidered and tied

Photo by Mert Carpenter

" I have integrated my background in painting
into my embellished quilts. I like to treat
the quilt as an unfinished canvas and keep
adding to it until it feels complete. I do lots of
drawings, some of which become designs for
art quilts. "

John W. Lefelhocz

WHAT KIND OF IMAGINATION conceives of sewing squares of aluminum flashing with weed-whacker cord to create an airplane silhouette that lights up? The mind of John W. Lefelhocz is behind this whimsical idea. Lefelhocz has also produced a piece composed of dollar bill facsimiles, some of which read "Perceive the Real Thing: Art and Greed Should Be Strangers." The viewer has to work to read the writing on this piece, because the words are covered by a huge painting of Monet's *Waterlilies*. Monet/money—get it? This kind of unusual juxtapositioning is typical of Lefelhocz. He creates intriguing images that draw the viewer in for a closer look at the details. One quilt features tiny tractors and little bags that say "Wild Oats." At first you think, "I get it: sowing wild oats," but then you wonder: "Maybe it's sewing wild oats?" And more questions follow: Why are there two elongated versions of Lefelhocz's face on this particular quilt? Why does he call this piece a self-portrait? Why do we expect that young men will sow wild oats? The jokes and puns are wonderful, and the questions linger.

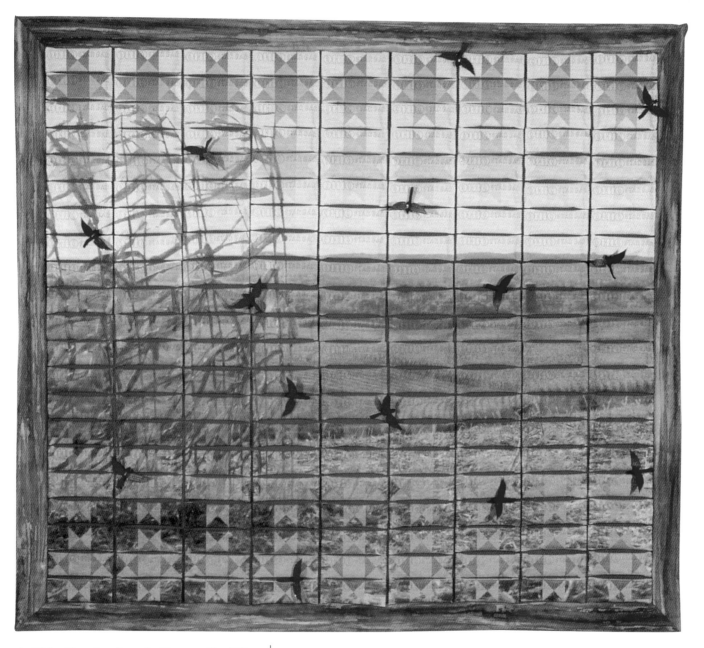

▲ Ohio Star Bar/Inspiration on the Wing | 2003

58 x 65 inches (1.5 x 1.7 m)

Cotton, tulle net, printed paper, feathers; hand sewn

Photos by T. Creamer

▲ Monet Over Money/No Boundaries | 1999

48 x 47 inches (1.2 x 1.2 m)
Fabric, nylon mesh, Czech, Japanese, German and Chinese beads, copper
wire, paper, clear transparency copies; machine and hand sewn

Photo by T. Creamer

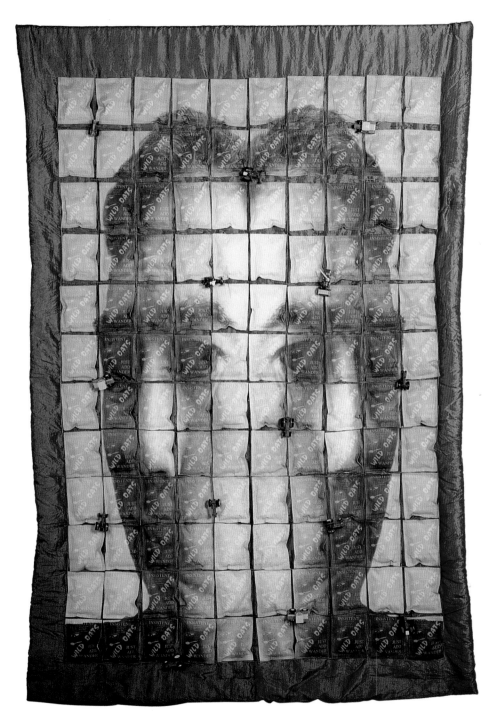

" When I first started out, I knew I wanted to make a quilt using nontraditional materials. I looked at the hardware store and the supermarket for interesting stuff to work with. I made my first art quilt using window screening and sugar packets. "

◀ **Two Faced/Sew (Sow) the Wild Oats** │ 2001

74 x 47 inches (1.9 x 1.2 m)
Fabric, printed paper, embroidery thread, toy tractors; machine and hand sewn

Photos by T. Creamer

▲ **Infernal Combustion** | 2002

36 x 36 inches (91.4 x 91.4 cm)
Kitchen matches, miniature gasoline cans,
fabric; machine and hand sewn, burned

Photos by T. Creamer

> " I still use everyday objects, but not exclusively. With quilt making, I think it's the layers that really get me moving in directions that other media don't. I think the physical layers somehow push me to think in narrative and metaphoric layers. "

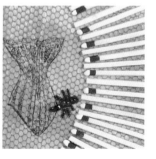

▲ Match Schticks | 2002

73 x 62 inches (1.9 x 1.6 m)
Kitchen matches (faux), paper, nylon net, satin, cotton, duck cloth,
peach skin fabric, rope, gemstone beads; machine and hand sewn
Photos by Brian Blauser

JOHN W. LEFELHOCZ

▲ Pure Harmony/American Abstract Expressionism
Travelers Cheques | 2006

51 x 73 inches (1.3 x 1.9 m)
Cotton, tulle net, printed paper, toy suitcase with quotes;
machine and hand sewn

Photos by T. Creamer

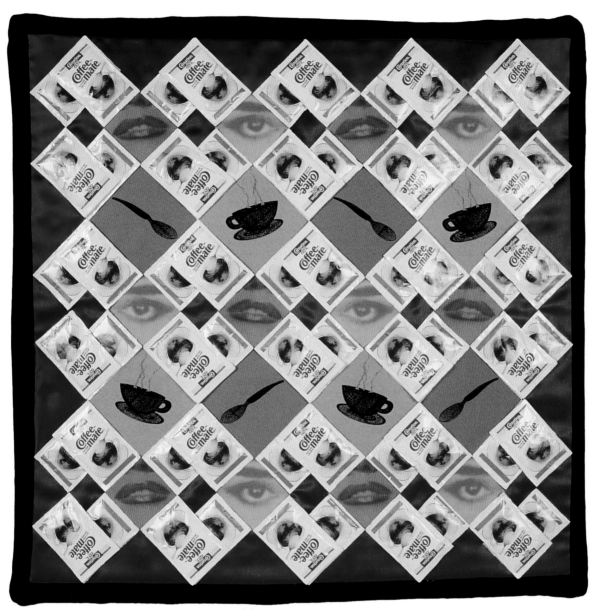

▲ **Tim and Jeanie's Wedding Quilt** | 2000

    24 x 24 inches (61 x 61 cm)
    Fabric, non-dairy creamer packets, paper;
    machine and hand sewn
    Photos by T. Creamer

◀ **Money for Nothing** | 1999

33 x 73 inches (83.8 x 185.4 cm)
Sugar packets, nylon window screening,
dental floss (mint flavored), green paper,
plastic flies; hand stitched

Photos by T. Creamer

▲ **Breaking the Barrier** | 2002

38 x 62 x 8 inches (96.5 x 157.5 x 20.3 cm)
Aluminum roof flashing, glass marbles, printed fabric, orange optic fiber (weed
whacker line), fluorescent lights, wood; hand painted, woven, drilled, sewn

Photos by T. Creamer

▲ **Ms. Ing Links** | 2004

35 x 56 inches (88.9 x 142.2 cm)
Cotton duck, glass Czech beads,
bicycle chain links, acrylic paint;
machine and hand sewn

Photos by T. Creamer

" I am a little intimidated by conventional fabric techniques. I am happiest making works that are very involved physically. I also enjoy making stuff that looks like one thing from far away, but up close becomes something else. "

Miriam Nathan-Roberts

HONORED IN JAPAN IN 2003 as one of the "thirty distinguished quilt artists of the world," Miriam Nathan-Roberts has been creating groundbreaking quilts since the beginning of the art-quilt movement. Her works that create an illusion of depth are particularly breathtaking. Creating the illusion of depth in two dimensions has fascinated her for years, partly because before getting corrective lenses at the age of 30, she had no depth perception. Nathan-Roberts' recent work is influenced by the new ability to use Photoshop to digitally manipulate and translate her photos of repeating shapes into concepts for quilts. Her celebration of form, pattern, and color is paired with a drive to experiment and explore that has filled 53 years of passionate creation of textile art.

▲ Changing Planes │ 1992

74 x 72 inches (1.9 x 1.8 m)

Cottons; machine pieced, appliquéd and quilted

Photos by artist

▲ **Spin Cycle** │ 1998

71 x 66 inches (1.8 x 1.7 m)

Commercial and hand-painted cotton; dyed, airbrushed, machine pieced, appliquéd, quilted

Photo by artist

▲ Cherries | 1998

57 x 57 inches (1.5 x 1.5 m)
Cotton, painter's canvas, polyester organza fabrics; hand
gessoed and painted, machine appliquéd and quilted

Photo by artist

" Over the past few years, I have been marrying digital art and digital printing with stitched and quilted textiles. I have completed several quilts based on photographed and scanned images, digitally manipulating the images with my computer. The final image is digitally printed on fabric with fiber-reactive dyes. "

▲ Cortland Street Subway Station | 2002
49 x 42 inches (1.3 x 1.1 m)
Cotton; digitally printed
Photo by artist

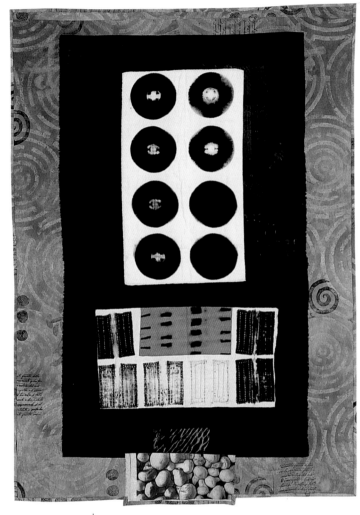

▲ Meditation | 2002

    49 x 34 inches (124.5 x 86.4 cm)
Cottons; discharged, machine
pieced and quilted

    Photos by artist

▲ Wine with Lichtenstein
   (A Toast to the New Millennium) | 2000

    62 x 42 inches (1.6 x 1.1 m)
Cottons; machine pieced and quilted

    Photo by artist

▲ Lattice Interweave | 1983

84 x 84 inches (2.1 x 2.1 m)
Cotton and cotton blends; machine pieced,
hand quilted by Sarah Hershberger

Photo by artist

" The art concepts I work
with include the relativity
of color; illusions of depth;
juxtaposition of elements;
playing with value; repeat
patterns; and creating
multiple visual planes on a
flat surface. All of my quilts
focus on these concepts,
though the images are
diverse. "

▲ **Temple Gate by Firelight** │ 2006

    52 x 40 inches (1.3 x 1 m)

    Cotton fabric, fiber-reactive dye; digitally printed

    Photo by artist

" My twin passions
for art and fabric
have found a home
in quilt making. My
approach to quilting
includes auditioning
an inordinate number
of fabrics for each
piece of the quilt. I
want people to be
intrigued enough to
take a second look
at my quilts, not just
walk by them. "

▲ **Letting Go** | 1985–1986
70 x 70 inches (1.8 x 1.8 m)
Cottons; hand dyed and painted, machine pieced,
hand quilted by artist and Sarah Hershberger
Photo by artist

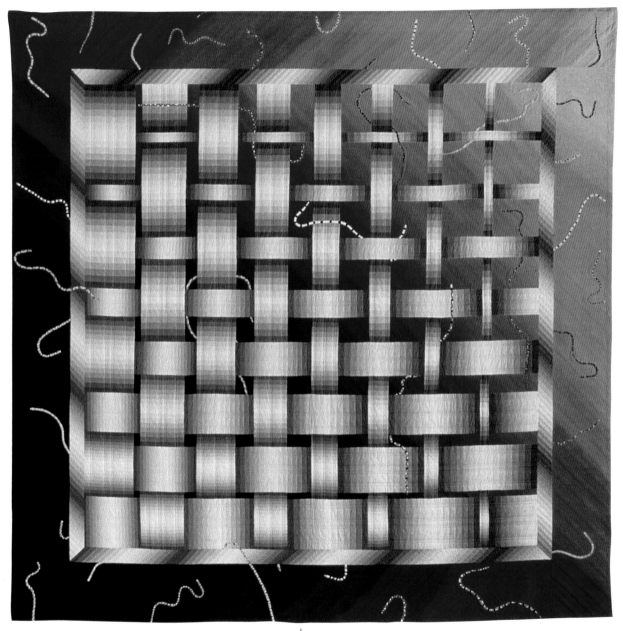

▲ **The Worms Crawl In–The Worms Crawl Out** | 1985–1986

103 x 103 inches (2.6 x 2.6 m)
Cottons; hand dyed, painted and appliquéd, machine pieced, hand quilted by Sarah Hershberger

Photo by artist

Jenny Hearn

A FULL SPECTRUM OF SATURATED COLOR flows through Jenny Hearn's work. Tiny squares of glowing jewel tones are pieced together into irregular and three-dimensional forms. Some of these forms are sculptural rather than flat. Some use recessed layers to create a sense of depth, and some make use of myriad individual elements that appear to have broken free of the boundaries of the traditional quilt form. The works are embellished with appliquéd geometric shapes—circles, squares, stars, and crescents—and then finished with embroidery. Hearn, a South African, works intuitively, letting the spirit of the fabric guide her in her exploration of Africa and its natural beauty. Working only with colors and textures available in commercial fabrics is a structure she finds freeing. In her more symbolic work, African stories, creatures, and symbols are arranged in formal grids. In her abstract work, Hearn is ruthless about color, which gives her works their power as the tones flow and pulsate across her surfaces.

▲ Pele | 2006

    65 x 72 inches (1.7 x 1.8 m)
    Commercial prints, hand-dyed silks, chiffons, cottons; machine pieced
    and appliquéd, hand and machine embroidered and quilted
    Photos by Dion Cuyler

" My work is about color—its moods, its psychological properties, and its ability to reinforce the 'storyline.' Color combinations create a rich background surface on which to set a theme. My themes are based on natural phenomena and the African tradition, as seen from a Eurocentric viewpoint. "

▲ **Flowering Fireworks** | 1994
65 x 54 inches (1.7 x 1.4 m)
Velvets, satins, lamé, voile, taffeta; free-standing appliquéd, hand embroidered, machine stitched, pieced and quilted
Photos by Dion Cuyler

JENNY HEARN

▲ Inca Gold | 1991

   45 x 36 inches (114.3 x 91.4 cm)
   Velvets, satins, lamé, taffeta, cotton,
   synthetic silks; hand embroidered,
   beadworked, machine stitched and pieced
   Photo by Dion Cuyler

▲ Fossil Pocket | 2000

   20 x 30 inches (50.8 x 76.2 cm)
   Commercial fabrics; hand and machine
   embroidered, machine pieced and quilted
   Photo by Dion Cuyler

" I work directly with the fabric, without preliminary drawing or preplanning other than the fabric selection. Although I admire the geometric qualities of conventional quilting, I find repetitive motifs restricting. I like to incorporate three-dimensional forms, knitting, and embroidery in a vibrant and improvisational way. "

▲ Moody Blues | 1999

60 x 48 inches (1.5 x 1.2 m)

Commercial prints; hand embroidered, machine pieced and quilted

Photos by Dion Cuyler

▲ Ol Doinyo Lengai | 2007

64 x 65 inches (1.6 x 1.7 m)
Commercial and hand-dyed fabrics; machine pieced, quilted
and appliquéd, hand and machine embroidered

Photos by Dion Cuyler

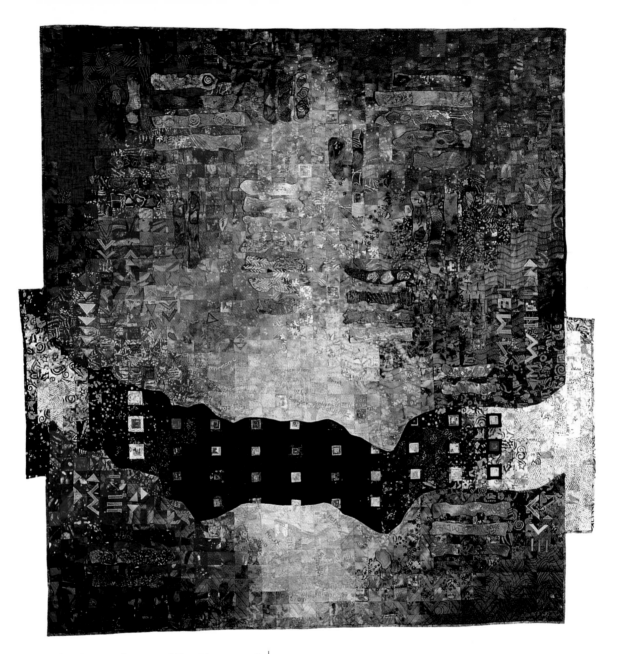

▲ **The Medium and the Message I** │ 2000

70 x 65 inches (1.8 x 1.7 m)

Commercial prints, hand-dyed silks; hand and machine embroidered, pieced, appliquéd and quilted

Photo by Dion Cuyler

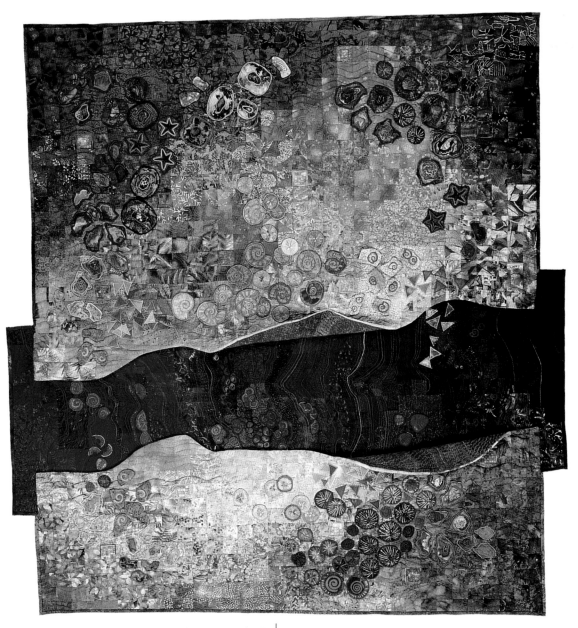

▲ Fissures, Fossils, and Fragments II | 2000

70 x 60 inches (1.8 x 1.5 m)
Commercial cottons, hand-dyed silks; hand embroidered,
machine embroidered, pieced, appliquéd and quilted

Photo by Dion Cuyler

" I let the fabric lead me in
a direction that makes
sense, rather than imposing
a preconceived design
on the material. In this
way, I create original and
spontaneous work. "

◀ **African Idiom I** | 2001
86⅝ x 48 inches (2.2 x 1.2 m)
Commercial and hand-dyed cottons;
machine embroidered, pieced and quilted
Photos by Heartquilt.com

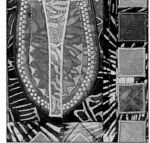

▲ African Idiom II | 2006

51½ x 47¼ inches (1.3 x 1.2 m)
Commercial print fabric; hand dyed, machine
pieced, appliquéd, embroidered and quilted

Photos by Dion Cuyler

Terrie Hancock Mangat

MEMORY JARS, MEMORIALS, AND NOSTALGIA all play into the visually exuberant imagery of Terrie Hancock Mangat's work. Collectively creating an autobiography of her life, Mangat's quilts often vibrate with the fierce energy of zigzag lightning bolts. Repeated shapes set up a staccato rhythm. Nothing is ever calm in her evocations of Catholic iconography, flea markets, Mexican shrines, and fireworks displays. Even in works depicting normally static objects, such as sticks, stones, or teapots, the images toss and tumble about the surface of her works in playful profusion. Often credited with pioneering and popularizing embellishment on contemporary quilts, Mangat produces appliquéd collages that combine pieced areas, painting, and embroidery. Her works often are nostalgic or memorial, but the emotions they evoke are more joyful than sad. Though the narrative content of each piece is based on Mangat's personal experiences, the responses they evoke are universal.

◀ **American Heritage Flea Market** | 1987

87 x 82 inches (2.2 x 2.1 m)
Cotton, silk, buttons, beads, paint, pipe cleaners; photo transferred, hand embroidered, reverse appliquéd, appliquéd

Photos by artist

▲ **Dashboard Saints: In Memory of St. Christopher**
(Who Lost His Magnetism) | 1985

100 x 150 inches (2.5 x 3.8 m)
Ribbons; photo transferred, hand embroidered, reverse
appliquéd, appliquéd, cut, hand quilted by Sue Rule

Photo by artist

▲ Shrine to the Beginning | 1988

101 x 96 inches (2.6 x 2.4 m)
Oil paint, linen canvas, cotton, beads, rosary, acrylic paint, metal St. Michael medal,
sequins; hand and reverse appliquéd, hand embroidered and quilted by Sue Rule

Photos by artist

" The things I do
quilts about are at
once personal and
universal. The viewers
can find meaning for
themselves in the work.
Every quilt I make is
about something I have
seen or experienced. "

▲ Sky Stones | 1987

98 x 88 inches (2.5 x 2.2 m)
Acrylic paint, cloth, sequins, hand-embroidered pieces
from Mexico, silk, cotton; reverse appliquéd

Photo by artist

▲ Cleveland Memorial Hospital
  Fireworks | 1993

> 85 x 120 inches (2.2 x 3 m)
> Cotton, silk, acrylic paint, beads;
> pieced, reverse appliquéd, hand
> embroidered
>
> Photo by Pam Monfort

◀ Memory Jars | 1988

> 36 x 50 inches (91.4 x 127 cm)
> Beads, buttons, cotton, lamé,
> rosary, commercial stickpin;
> reverse appliquéd
>
> Photo by artist

▲ **Mexican Graveyard** | 1986

106 x 86 inches (2.7 x 2.2 m)

Beads, buttons, ribbons, sequins, oil paint, linen canvas appliques; hand embroidered, appliquéd, reverse appliquéd, machine pieced, photo transferred, hand quilted by Sue Rule

Photos by artist

▲ Hancock Memorial Quilt | 1993

102 x 93 inches (2.6 x 2.4 m)
Beads, buttons, tie, felted wool, oil quilt piece; appliquéd and reverse appliquéd, photo silk screen-printed, hand embroidered, decoupaged
Photo by artist

" Many people who don't normally look at art enjoy a good quilt show, because it calls to their soul—the comfort of cloth, the richness of color, and then the option of sequins, beads, layers of sheer fabrics, and thread laid in next to paint. "

MANGAT

TERRIE HANCOCK

▲ Lauryn Visits Baha | 2000
40 x 30 inches (101.6 x 76.2 cm)
Hand-printed fabric; bargello pieced, hand embroidered
Photo by artist

▲ Sacred Heart Garden | 1988

　　96 x 91 inches (2.4 x 2.3 m)
　　Paint, beads, zippers, silk, cotton, oil paint,
　　linen; reverse appliquéd
　　Photos by artist

Wendy Huhn

WHAT A WICKED SENSE OF HUMOR Wendy Huhn has. Lifelong inspiration has come from an early love of paper dolls, but her work juxtaposes those childlike images with a host of more ominous ones. Skeletons, guns, tourniquets, and knives interact with fifties-style images of housewives, children, and teddy bears. Huhn's work leaves the viewer constantly off balance, looking for the menace behind the façade. Based on an immense library of photocopied images, Huhn's quilts include a variety of printing processes to transfer her icons onto cloth. While her recent work is also heavily embellished with a vast assortment of sequins and beads, the central elements remain what engage the viewer in puzzling out the story behind the relationship of the main figures: What is the joke? Should I be amused, angered, or aware? Why are the pigs eating the wolf?

▲ Somnambulist | 2003

72 x 82 inches (1.8 x 2.1 m)

Canvas, vintage fabrics, netting, heat transfers, phosphorescent medium, monofilament, beads; stenciled, painted, machine quilted, bound

Photos by David Loveall Photography

▲ **Eat** | 2006

60 x 48 inches (1.5 x 1.2 m)

Canvas, heat transfers, phosphorescent medium, monofilament, beads;
screen-printed, painted, sanded, machine quilted, bound

Photos by David Loveall Photography

◀ Save the Last Dance... | 2001

68 x 44 inches (1.7 x 1.1 m)
Cotton, paint, stencils, heat transfers,
beads, photocopy fabric; air brushed,
machine quilted, bound

Photos by artist

WENDY HUHN

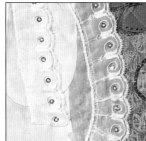

▲ Silent Killer | 1999

72 x 64 inches (1.8 x 1.6 m)

Canvas printed with bubble wrap, heat transfers, glue transfers, vintage apron, beads, monofilament; machine quilted, bound

Photos by David Loveall Photography

◀ **How I Won Him: By a Blonde** | 1997

28 x 37 inches (71.1 x 94 cm)
Cotton, photocopy fabric, stencils, heat transfers,
monofilament; painted, machine quilted
Photos by David Loveall Photography

Girl Talk | 1998 ▶

45 x 53 inches (1.1 x 1.4 m)
Canvas, heat transfers, plastic lace, ribbon, gar-
ter belt clips, sequins, monofilament; screen-
printed, painted, airbrushed, machine quilted,
bound
Photos by artist

WENDY HUHN

▲ **Not a Job for Grownups** | 2004

60 x 62 inches (1.5 x 1.6 m)
Cotton, heat transfers, phosphorescent medium, monofilament,
beads; screen-printed, painted, machine quilted, bound

Photos by David Loveall Photography

" What I'm attempting to do in my work is present to the viewer an abundance of information. I am a scavenger of visual imagery. I borrow imagery from nineteenth- and twentieth-century magazines and books to alter and reassemble. In my 'borrowing,' my intent is to honor the image as well as the source that produced it. "

▲ Sleep | 2007

60 x 48 inches (1.5 x 1.2 m)
Canvas, netting, monofilament, beads; screen-printed, painted, sanded, machine quilted, airbrushed, bound

Photos by David Loveall Photography

WENDY HUHN

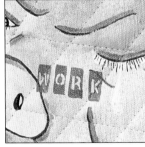

▲ Work | 2006

63 x 48 inches (1.6 x 1.2 m)
Canvas, paint, stencils, transfers, vintage fabrics, beads; painted, sanded, xylene
and heat stamping, phosphorescent medium, machine quilted, bound

Photos by David Loveall Photography

" As a child I was obsessed with creating my own paper dolls. I would cut and paste together my own creations from magazines. I would reconstruct the pieces to create my own paper people. This is how I continue to work—foraging, cutting, pasting, enlarging, reducing, and waiting for the images to speak. "

▲ **Betrayal** | 2000

57 x 48 inches (1.5 x 1.2 m)
Cotton, heat transfers, netting, beads, monofilament;
painted, stenciled, machine quilted, bound

Photos by David Loveall Photography

B.J. Adams

"MY HANDS ARE THE PRIMARY TOOLS for all the techniques I use in my artwork, as well as in daily life," says B.J. Adams, and much of her work features incredibly realistic-looking hands and tools created through detailed machine embroidery. Gently humorous vignettes show hands placing objects or handling painting or needlework tools as they work to create the images of her pieces. Sometimes the hands seem to hold up the piece for our inspection; other times they reach out to communicate across boundaries. A lover of puns, Adams seeks connections among the groups of objects she portrays. While the alphabet series ostensibly groups objects by their initial letter, the choices display additional connections, such as the similarity of shape in the butterflies, bows, and bananas in *Variations on "B."* That the bananas vary from ripe to blackened over-ripeness is yet another instance of Adams' humor—"black" is also a B word. Lovingly detailed trees, chairs, flowers, birds, telephones, and abstract forms populate Adams' work, but her hands are always present in each series she creates.

▲ **Contemplating Chaos** | 2006

40 x 57 inches (1 x 1.5 m)
Cotton, canvas, paint, thread; free-motion
machine embroidered, quilted

Photos by PRS Associates

▲ **Variations on "B"** | 2002

42 x 42 inches (1.1 x 1.1 m)
Painted canvas, cotton, paint, thread, buttons, bows;
free-motion machine embroidered, appliquéd, quilted

Photo by PRS Associates

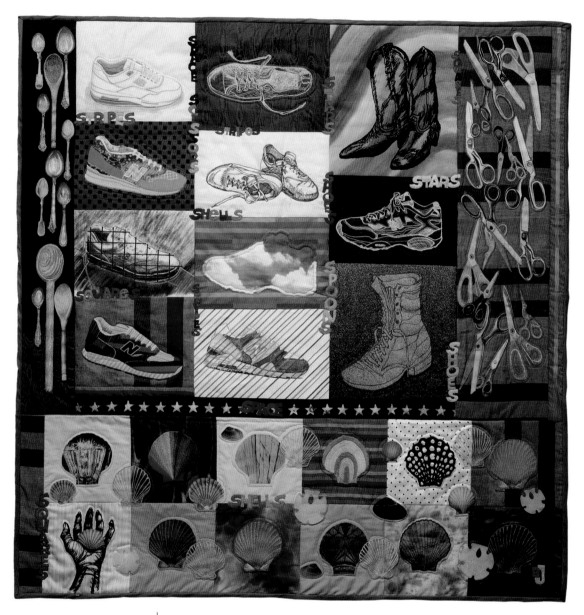

▲ **Variations on "S"** | 2002

53 x 52 inches (1.4 x 1.3 m)
Cotton fabrics, acrylic paint, heat transfers, thread;
free-motion machine embroidered, pieced, quilted

Photo by PRS Associates

▲ A Classical Palette | 1999

31½ x 40½ inches (80 x 102.9 cm)
Cotton, painted canvas, thread;
free-motion machine
embroidered, quilted

Photo by PRS Associates

" My artwork began with representation, developed into
abstraction, and now goes back and forth between the two,
sometimes combining elements of both as well as of surrealism.
I want the realistic or surrealistic work to give the viewer a
surprise—an out-of-context image, size, or viewpoint. "

▲ **A Seasonal Spectrum** | 2000

21 x 55½ inches (53.3 x 141 cm)
Painted canvas, cotton, silk, thread; free-motion machine embroidered, quilted

Photo by PRS Associates

◀ **Variations on "L"** | 2002

33 x 31 inches (83.8 x 78.7 cm)
Painted canvas, heat transfers, paint, thread; free-motion machine embroidered, appliquéd, quilted

Photo by PRS Associates

▲ Gossip | 2006

25½ x 38 inches (64.8 x 96.5 cm)
Cotton, canvas, paint, heat transfers, thread; free-motion machine embroidered, appliquéd, quilted

Photo by PRS Associates

" While working on one piece, another idea often emerges. This constant, stimulating flow causes my work to evolve. The unusual or commonplace materials and techniques I use, the focus required by the slow process of this art, and the infinite subjects available keep my work ever changing, challenging, and always motivating. "

▲ **Conversations** | 2006

30 x 40 inches (76.2 x 101.6 cm)
Painted canvas, cotton fabric, thread, colored pencil; free-motion
machine embroidered, appliquéd, quilted

Photos by PRS Associates

▲ **Sitting Still, Life** │ 2007

37 x 39 inches (94 x 99.1 cm)
Cotton denim, upholstery fabrics, thread; free-motion
machine embroidered, pieced

Photos by PRS Associates

" Art quilts are an extension of my drawing and painting. My love of texture is the primary reason I moved off paper and canvas and onto fabric. The sewing machine became my brush, hundreds of colors of thread have become my paint, and textiles are my 'support,' to use a painting term. "

▲ **Three Trees at Home** | 2006
22 x 46 inches (55.9 x 116.8 cm)
Old towels, cotton fabric, thread; free-motion machine embroidered, appliquéd, quilted
Photo by PRS Associates

Inge Mardal & Steen Hougs

HUSBAND AND WIFE TEAM Steen Hougs and Inge Mardal both have professional backgrounds in engineering, mechanics, and electronics. This bent toward precision also comes through in their artwork, which is meticulously composed. While photographs of natural subjects—particularly birds, butterflies, and rock formations—inspire much of their work, their recent pieces also have explored architectural vignettes encountered in their travels. They refine each composition down to its essence. The image is translated into a whole-cloth painting by Hougs, then embellished with rows upon rows of close quilting lines by Mardal. Mardal and Hougs, who are both Danish, say they are drawn to the extremely tactile nature of quilting, the way in which quilting lines create a low relief across the surface, and the fashion in which fabric absorbs ambient light. The immediacy of their imagery is what draws viewers to their art.

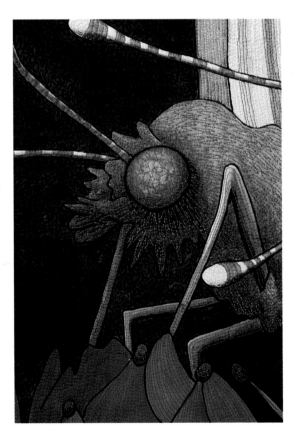

◀ **Twilight Rendezvous** | 2002

80 x 60½ inches (2 x 1.5 m)
Cotton, thread, fabric paint, whole
cloth; hand painted, machine quilted

Photos by P. Leemans

" Our initial way of designing with and in fabrics gradually developed into a more painterly approach, in which selected fabrics formed the palettes for the motifs. Searching for a higher level of autonomy, we took full control of values, hues, gradations, and other elements by basing our works on whole-cloth painted foundations augmented by subsequent quilting. "

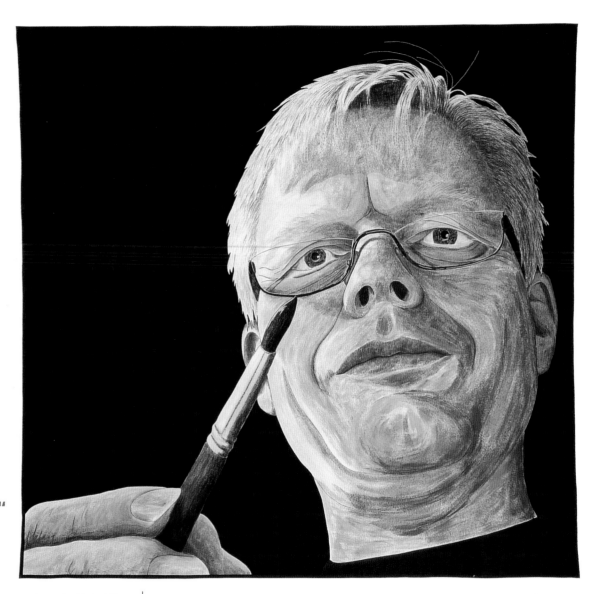

▲ Palette's View | 2005

50¾ x 50¾ inches (1.3 x 1.3 m)

Cotton, thread, fabric paint, whole cloth; hand painted, machine quilted

Photo by P. Leemans

▲ **Inviting** | 2006

51 x 51 inches (1.3 x 1.3 m)

Cotton, thread, fabric paint, whole cloth; hand painted, machine quilted

Photo by P. Leemans

▲ **Moulting** │ 2002

55 x 74¾ inches (1.4 x 1.9 m)

Cotton, thread, fabric paint, whole cloth; hand painted, machine quilted

Photo by P. Leemans

▲ **River of Life** │ 2005

66 x 65½ inches (1.7 x 1.7 m)

Cotton, thread, fabric paint, whole cloth; hand painted, machine quilted

Photo by P. Leemans

▲ **Against the Wind** | 1999

50½ x 61½ inches (1.3 x 1.6 m)
Cotton, thread; hand appliquéd,
machine pieced and quilted
Photo by Steen Hougs

◀ Ringed | 2005

84¾ x 65¾ inches (2.2 x 1.7 m)
Cotton, thread, fabric paint, whole cloth;
hand painted, machine quilted

Photos by P. Leemans

Aware | 2002 ▶

83 x 83 inches (2.1 x 2.1 m)
Cotton, thread, fabric paint, whole cloth;
hand painted, machine quilted

Photo by P. Leemans

▲ **Gulls in the Heat Haze** | 2004

51 x 77 inches (1.3 x 2 m)
Cotton, thread, fabric paint, whole cloth;
hand painted, machine quilted

Photos by P. Leemans

" We find the quilted form encourages working in large formats, but at the same time it poses tremendous challenges on design and communication of artistic expressions. "

◄ Nature's View | 2005
50¾ x 50¾ inches
(1.3 x 1.3 m)
Cotton, thread, fabric
paint, whole cloth; hand
painted, machine quilted
Photo by P. Leemans

Chiaki Dosho

ARTISTS ARE OFTEN DRIVEN to capture the impossible. For Japanese artist Chiaki Dosho, finding ways to depict petals of cherry blossoms fluttering in the sky has been an obsession for many years. Striving to create the sensation of movement in an inherently motionless medium has led Dosho to explore many different techniques: swirling lines of quilting, curved piecing, and flowing couched embellishment. Most recently she has developed a pointillist approach achieved by overlapping tiny cut pieces, petals of fabric that quiver in the slightest breath of air. Her works in this series also incorporate windows, supported only by fine vertical threads, through which one views the petals drifting downward. Cherry blossoms have layers of meaning in Japanese culture, and Dosho tries to capture their essence through her layers of fabric. Her delicate colors and tiny pieces convey the fragility of the falling cherry blossoms and the ephemeral quality of all life.

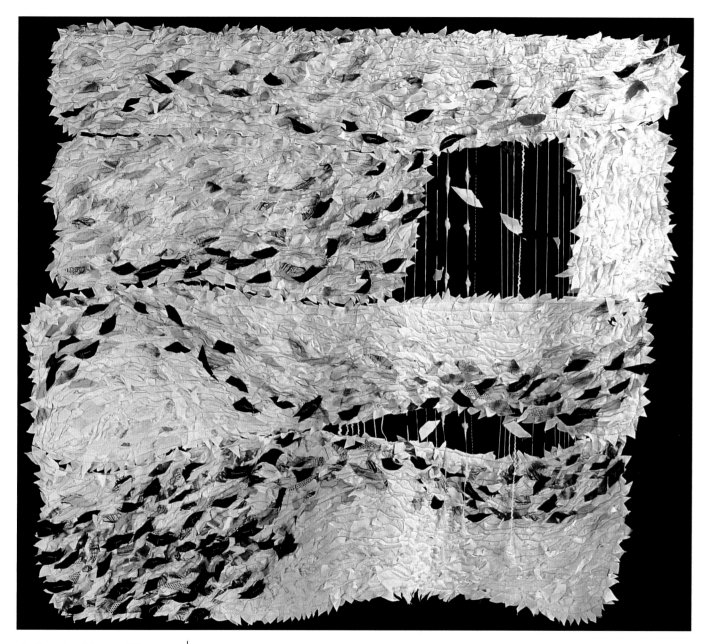

▲ **Sumie–Cherry Blossom** | 2006

59 x 67 inches (1.5 x 1.7 m)

Old Japanese silk kimono; direct appliquéd, machine quilted, coated

Photos by Daisuke A.

" My first art quilt was based on the ideas of established paintings and craft works. Since then, I have worked with my own ideas and now use a direct appliqué technique of my invention. "

▲ **The Light in the Morning Mist** | 1989

86½ x 71 inches (2.2 x 1.8 m)
Cotton, synthetic fiber cloth, wool rope; pieced, hand quilted and appliquéd
Photo by J. Sekiguchi

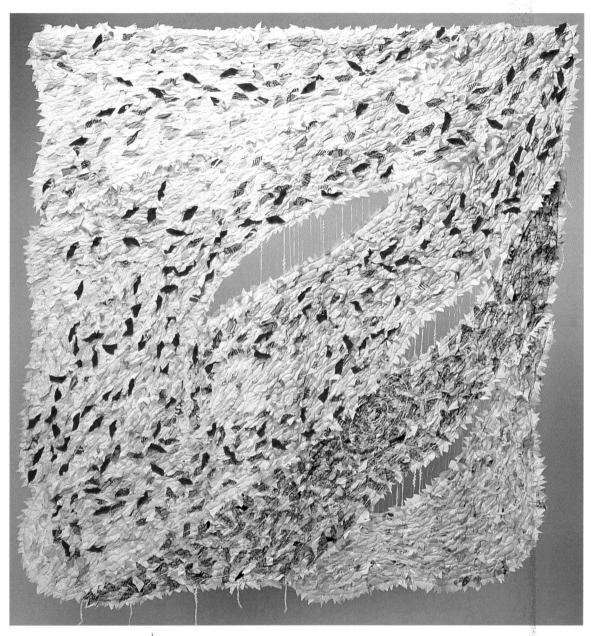

▲ **Cherry Blossom V** | 2006

82¾ x 78¾ inches (2.1 x 2 m)
Old Japanese silk kimono; direct appliqué, machine quilted, coated

Photo by T. Kobe

▲ **Bubble II** | 2004

83 x 68½ inches (2.1 x 1.8 m)
Old Japanese silk kimono; pieced, machine quilted, coated

Photos by T. Kobe

▲ Reflecting Fish in the Sea | 2004

86½ x 70 inches (2.2 x 1.8 m)
Old Japanese cotton kimono;
machine quilted, coated

Photo by Daisuke A.

▲ R & B | 2005

52 x 41¾ inches (1.3 x 1.1 m)
Old Japanese silk kimono; direct appliquéd,
coated, torn, machine quilted

Photo by Daisuke A.

CHIAKI DOSHO

▲ Illusion VII Sound III | 2002

86½ x 82¾ inches (2.2 x 2.1 m)
Old Japanese silk/wool kimono; hand appliquéd
Photo by Daisuke A.

▲ **Wind I** | 2004

76 x 75 inches (1.9 x 1.9 m)
Old Japanese silk kimono; direct appliquéd, machine quilted, hand stitched
Photo by T. Kobe

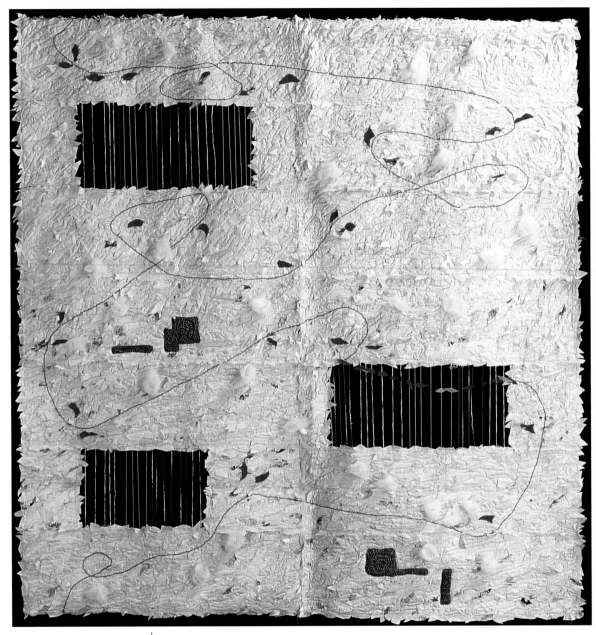

▲ **Cherry Blossom II** | 2006

78¾ x 78¾ inches (2 x 2 m)

Old Japanese silk kimono; direct appliquéd, machine quilted, coated

Photo by Daisuke A.

" For me, making quilts is a means of self-expression. My attempts to free myself from stereotypes are key to creating my quilts. New ideas can be found in paintings, music, and nature—all of these areas provide me with ways to brush up on my skills. "

◀ **Cherry Blossom** | 2005
59 x 45¼ inches (1.5 x 1.2 m)
Old Japanese silk kimono;
direct appliquéd, machine
quilted, coated
Photos by T. Kobe

Inge Hueber

"TRANSFORMING PASSING TIME into a visible object" is how Inge Hueber describes the experience of creating her artwork. While her early work focused on her invented variations on Seminole piecing, Hueber's recent work uses the nine-patch block as its inspiration, but replaces the usual square pieces with stripes. Certainly no one would mistake the German artist's quilts for traditional designs: The palette of her own hand-dyed cottons, her rhythmic color placement, and her use of visible seams as embellishment mark these as contemporary works of art. In *Nine-Patch Variation*, Hueber pushes the concept of a quilt further by creating a top of transparent cotton organza and using the layer of air between the organza and the pieced layer as the middle layer instead of batting. Saying that she invents what she feels, Hueber uses the placement of color in her geometric creations to express how she sees the rhythm of life. The use of strip piecing expresses her approach to life—simple, straightforward, and full of verve.

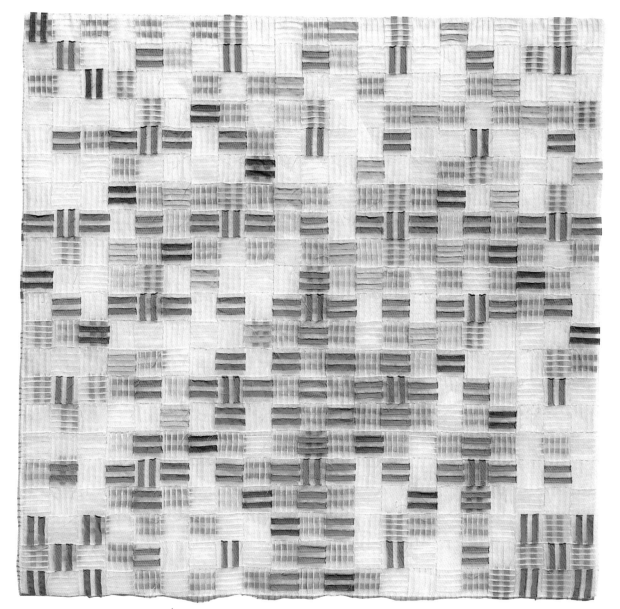

▲ Nine-Patch Variation | 2004
64 x 64 inches (1.6 x 1.6 m)
Cotton, cotton organza; hand dyed, machine pieced
Photos by Roland Hueber

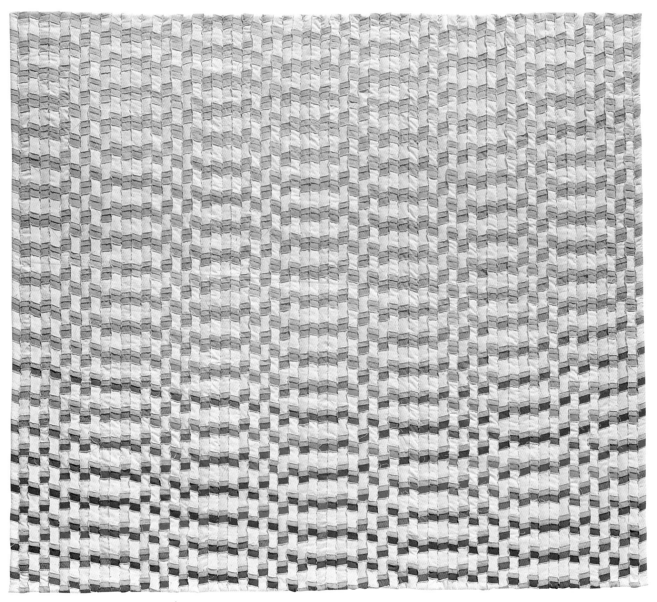

▲ **In Pursuit of Happiness** | 2006

74 x 83 inches (1.9 x 2.1 m)
Cotton; hand dyed, machine pieced and quilted

Photos by Roland Hueber

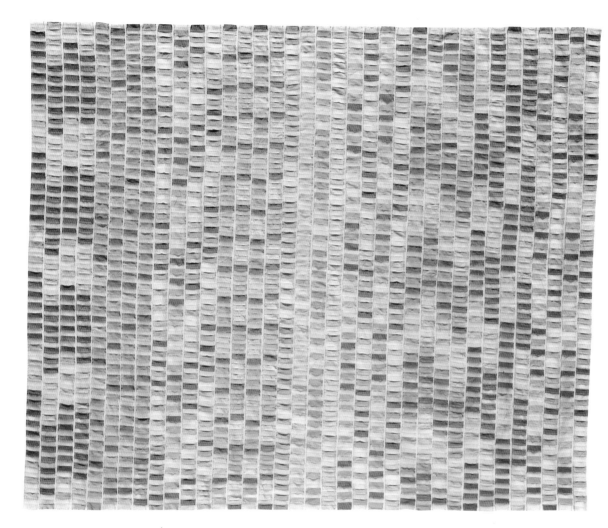

" From the beginning, I have dyed all my material, and I have learned a lot about the special language of colored cloth. I am still fascinated and often surprised by the quilting process—for example, realizing the potential of visible seams to add texture and depth. "

▲ Transparent Songs | 2004
   59 x 69 inches (1.5 x 1.8 m)
   Cotton; hand dyed, machine pieced and quilted
   Photos by Roland Hueber

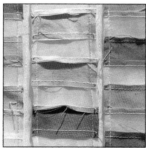

" My quilts are a technical construction on one hand, and a combination of emotional colors on the other. I am searching for a balance between textile flexibility, color values, intuition, and precise craftsmanship. "

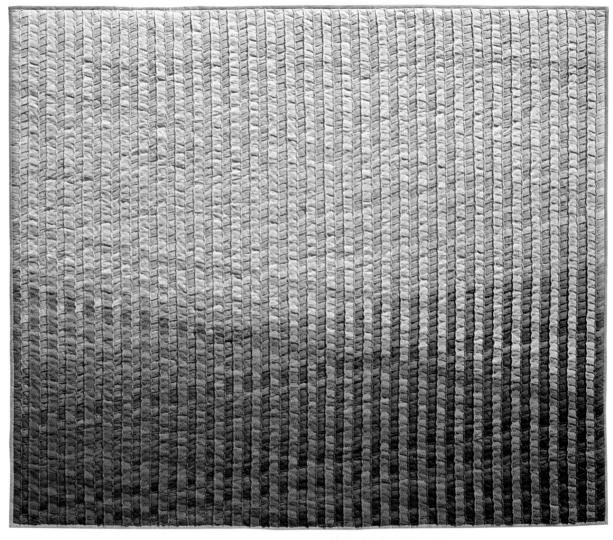

▲ **Late Summer** │ 1991

58 x 69 inches (1.5 x 1.8 m)
Cotton; hand dyed, machine pieced and quilted
Photos by Roland Hueber

▲ **Summer 2001** | 2001

72 x 91 inches (1.8 x 2.3 m)
Cotton; hand dyed, machine pieced and quilted

Photo by Roland Hueber

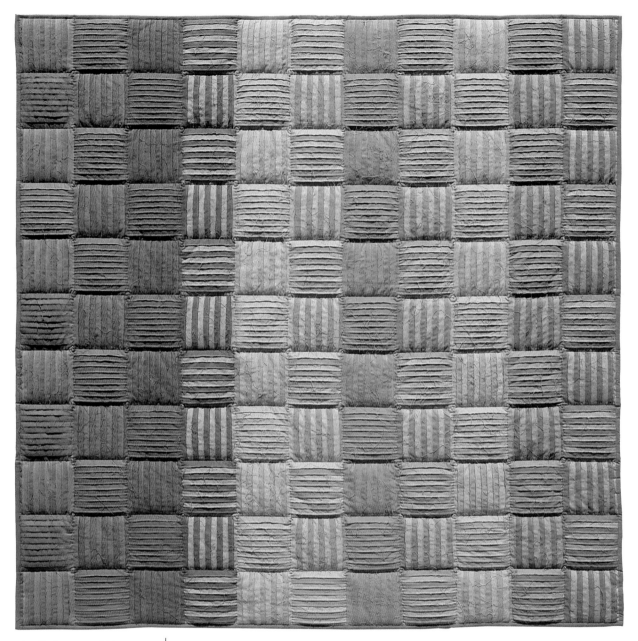

▲ **Stripes and Squares** | 1995

66 x 67 inches (1.7 x 1.7 m)

Cotton; hand dyed, machine pieced and quilted

Photo by Roland Hueber

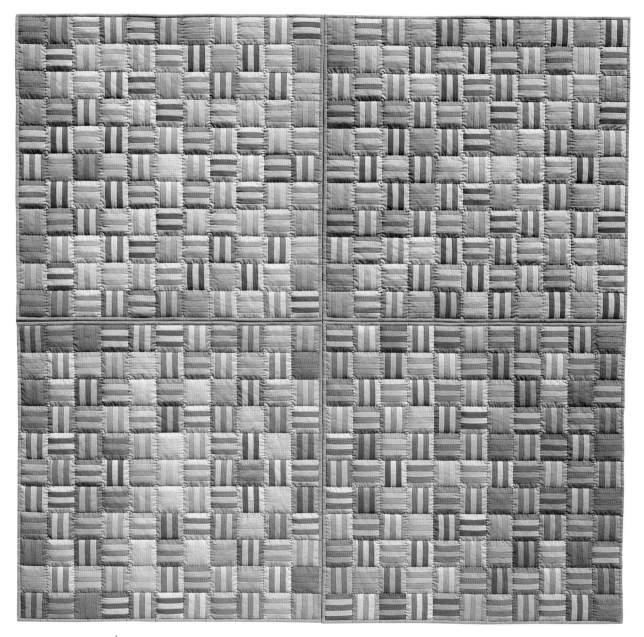

▲ **Farben Lust** | 1996

Each quadrant, 32 x 32 inches (81.3 x 81.3 cm)
Cotton; hand dyed, machine pieced and quilted

Photo by Roland Hueber

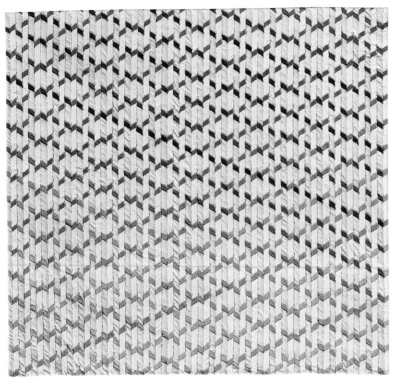

◀ **In Full Swing** │ 2006

70 x 73 inches (1.8 x 1.9 m)
Cotton; hand dyed, machine pieced and quilted

Photos by Roland Hueber

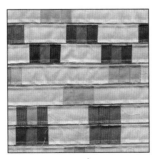

Serendipity II │ 2003 ▶

51 x 67 inches (1.3 x 1.7 m)
Cotton; hand dyed, machine
pieced and quilted

Photos by Roland Hueber

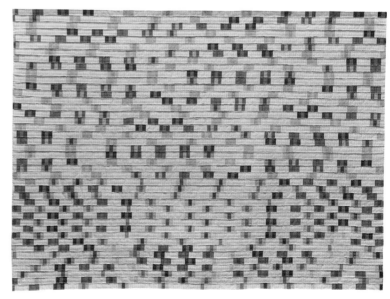

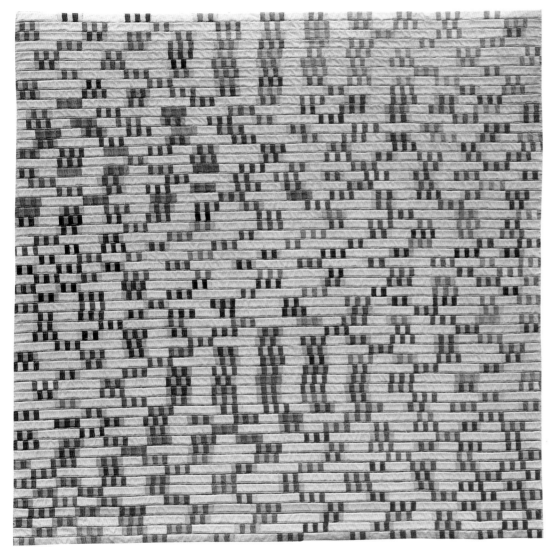

" My quilts have
developed into a kind
of visual diary. I cannot
plan changes—they
occur when they are
due, just as in real life.
Making quilts has given
me a key to my own
life, a key to open doors
that would have been
locked otherwise. "

▲ Serendipity I │ 2003
66 x 66 inches (1.7 x 1.7 m)
Cotton; hand dyed, machine pieced and quilted
Photos by Roland Hueber

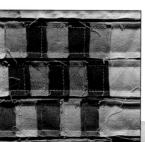

Michael James

AFTER MORE THAN 20 YEARS OF EXPLORING the infinite variations possible in manipulating pieced stripe forms, Michael James completely changed his style. In 2002 he began working with digitally developed and printed fabric to explore iconic figures and patterns drawn from historic sources. The ability to incorporate photographic elements and to manipulate them using design software has led him to fabric surfaces that hold a different kind of narrative and expressive meaning. He says he is interested in representing "the idea of dual realities existing side by side or within one another." For a metaphysically inclined thinker, this new way of working allows James to broaden the poetic resonance of his work. While some of this work references traditional patchwork and his older style of design, most of it is starkly simple in its structure and focuses instead on the meanings inherent in the emotional core around which the work is conceived and organized.

▲ Ghost Figure | 2005

36½ x 78½ inches (92.7 x 199.4 cm)
Cotton, reactive dyes; digitally developed and
printed, machine sewn

Photos by Larry Gawel

▲ **Interference Effect: (Betrayed) Lover's Knot** | 2005

52 x 80½ inches (1.3 x 2.1 m)
Cotton; digitally developed and printed, machine
pieced and quilted

Photos by Larry Gawel

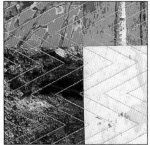

MICHAEL AMES

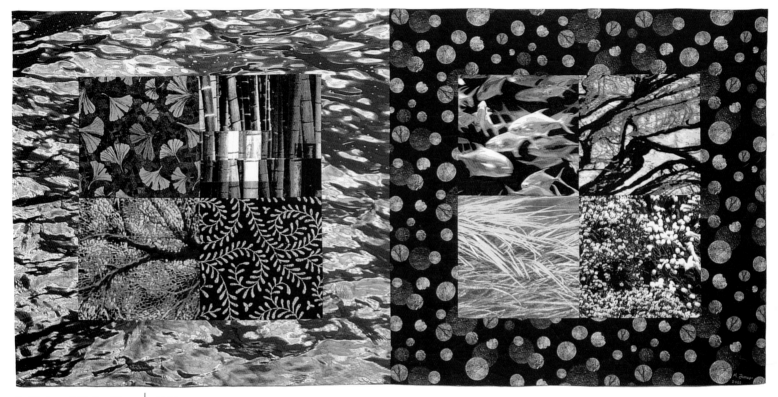

▲ **Natural Selection** | 2003

41 x 82½ inches (1 x 2.1 m)
Cotton, reactive dyes; digitally
developed and printed, machine
pieced and quilted

Photo by Larry Gawel

❝ I value fabric as the richly expressive material that it is. Its drape

and hang make it the ideal complement to the human body, and

that flexibility is something that I feel is integral to what a fabric

construction such as a quilt is. ❞

▲ Sky/Wind Variations II │ 1990

51 x 86 inches (1.3 x 2.2 m)
Cotton, silk; machine pieced and quilted

Photos by David Caras

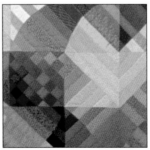

◀ Rhythm/Color: Improvisation 2 │ 1986

79 x 79 inches (2 x 2 m)
Cotton, silk; machine pieced and quilted

Photos by David Caras

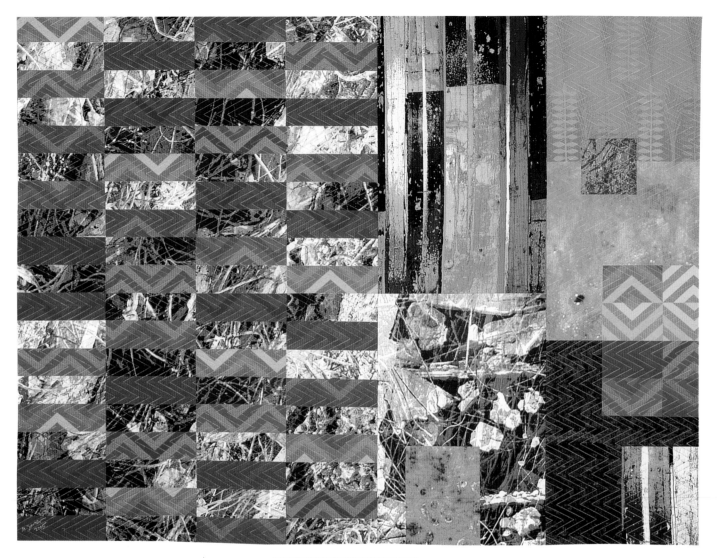

▲ **Abstraction #6: Afterimage** | 2005

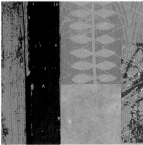

55½ x 72½ inches (1.4 x 1.8 m)
Cotton; digitally developed and printed,
machine pieced and quilted

Photos by Larry Gawel

▲ **The Metaphysics of Action (Entropic Forms)** | 1994

101 x 101 inches (2.6 x 2.6 m)

Cotton, silk; machine pieced and quilted

Photo by David Caras

" Through the development of my work over the last few years, I've sustained an interest in representing—either figuratively or expressively—the proverbial 'two sides of the same coin,' the idea of dual realities existing side by side or within one another. "

▲ The Nature of Truth (The Truth of Nature) | 2003
    49 x 109 inches (1.3 x 2.8 m)
    Cotton; digitally developed and printed, machine pieced and quilted
    Photos by Larry Gawel

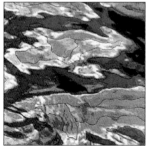

▲ **Momentum** | 2003

52 x 87 inches (1.3 x 2.2 m)
Cotton; digitally developed and printed,
machine pieced and quilted

Photo by Larry Gawel

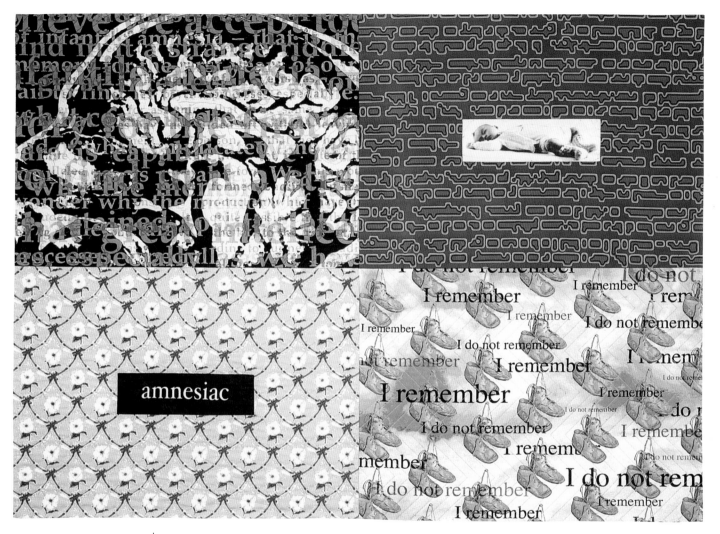

▲ **A Strange Riddle 3** | 2002

35¼ x 48½ inches (89.5 x 123.2 cm)

Cotton; digitally developed and printed, machine pieced and quilted

Photo by Larry Gawel

Velda E. Newman

OVERSIZED SCALE IS VELDA E. NEWMAN'S SIGNATURE. Her flowers are huge. So are her fish, shells, and butterflies. By creating pieces of such large dimensions, Newman offers viewers the chance to look closely at the wondrous beauty of the natural forms that surround us. Her appliquéd creations are often made from her own hand-dyed fabrics, which she bleaches, inks, paints, and stipple quilts to create a portrait of heightened realism. Color is her passion and often dictates her choice of subject matter. Placing the saturated reds and acid greens of geraniums against an electric blue background makes the image vibrate with color. The use of black and white pieced graphic elements and borders grounds Newman's work, giving the eye places to rest. Her portraits attempt to capture the essence of each subject, aiming not for photorealism, but for a kind of archetypal image that truly celebrates nature's beauty.

▲ Nasturtium | 1987

96 x 90 inches (2.4 x 2.3 m)
Cotton; hand dyed, appliquéd and quilted
Photos by Steve Buckley

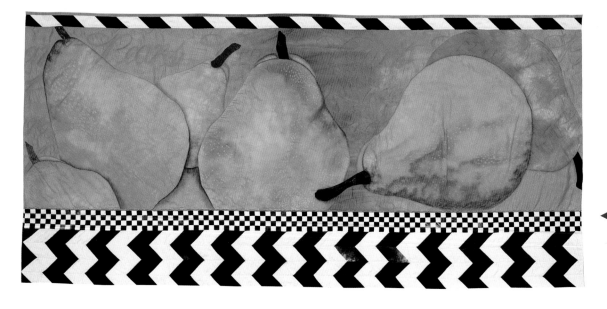

◀ Six Pears │ 2003

60 x 107 inches (1.5 x 2.7 m)
Cotton sateen, paint, resist;
hand dyed
Photo by Steve Buckley

▲ Sunflower │ 1996

56 x 120 inches (1.4 x 3.1 m)
Cottons, ink, paint; hand dyed
Photo by Steve Buckley

" Most of my work is realistic, based on my own photos or pictures from books. I begin with my own hand-dyed fabric and incorporate other media, like paint, ink, and resist. The versatility these media offer in conjunction with the craftsmanship of quilt making continues to be both challenging and rewarding for me. "

▲ Sea Shells | 2002

60 x 142 inches (1.5 x 3.6 m)

Cotton sateen, pencil and pastel; hand dyed, painted

Photo by Steve Buckley

▲ Baskets │ 2000

42 x 44 inches (1.1 x 1.2 m)
Canvas, paint, ink, crayons, pencil

Photo by Steve Buckley

▲ Bass: In Your Dreams | 1999

79 x 86 inches (2 x 2.2 m)
Cotton, foil, paint, ink; hand dyed
Photo by Steve Buckley

VELDA E. NEWMAN

375

▲ **Freedom Is Fragile** | 1986

72 x 72 inches (1.8 x 1.8 m)
Cottons; hand stitched and quilted

Photo by Steve Buckley

" Somewhere in the working process, my vision skews—colors become bolder, shapes and subjects get larger. It is through this use of exaggerated colors and shapes that I hope to inspire the viewer and celebrate the beauty and spectacle of Mother Nature. "

▲ Geranium | 1993

80 x 98 inches (2 x 2.5 m)
Cottons, ink; discharged, hand stitched, dyed and quilted

Main photo by Ken Burris, courtesy of John M. Walsh III; detail by Steve Buckley

▲ Hydrangea | 1989

84 x 99 inches (2.1 x 2.5 m)

Cotton; discharged, hand stitched, dyed and quilted

Main photo by Ken Burris, courtesy of John M. Walsh III;
detail by Steve Solinsky

" I find nature to be an endless source of inspiration, and I suppose my life on the shores and in the mountains of California has influenced me most. When I work, I begin conventionally, by breaking down a design into its most basic elements of shape and color. "

▲ Hollyhocks | 2001

62 x 107 inches (1.6 x 2.7 m)
Silk face, cotton sateen backing and binding,
pencil and pastel; hand dyed, painted
Photos by Steve Buckley

Anne Woringer

AN EXPERT ON MEDIEVAL FABRICS, Anne Woringer often uses antique linen and hemp fabrics in her work. Woringer dyes these fabrics, which were hand-spun and woven in the nineteenth century, to create a very different look from what is possible with contemporary textiles. She likens their muted and sober colors to those of the Amish quilts that first inspired her passion for quilting. Woringer, who is from France, constantly experiments with the use of color, light, and technique to find ways to bring more spontaneity and gaiety to her design process. A fascination with visual puzzles has led to a large body of work that references mazes, labyrinths, and optical illusions. The interplay of positive and negative shapes in her work echoes her interest in the visual rhythm of writing, which she feels is similar to the rhythm of stitching. Recently Woringer has been using shibori discharge of black and indigo fabrics to create "unpredictable, mysterious marks," which she highlights with embroidery. Throughout her work, what is most evident is Woringer's love and respect for the fabrics themselves.

▲ Les Sentiers Vagabonds | 2006

59 x 59 inches (1.5 x 1.5 m)
Thai hemp; noi shibori discharged,
hand embroidered and quilted

Photos by Bruno Jarret

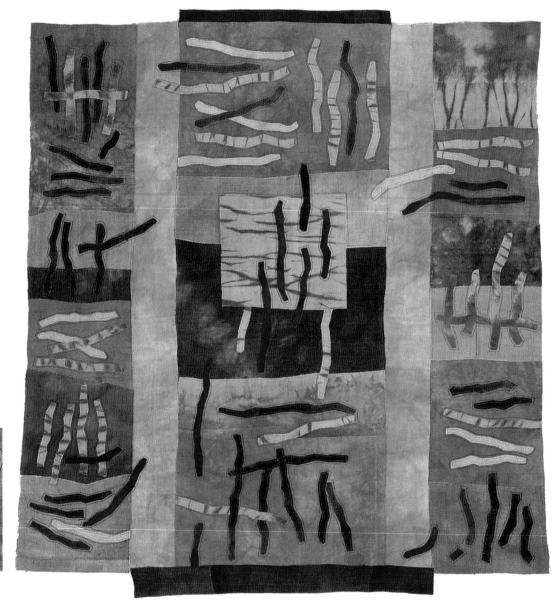

▲ Les Bois Flottés | 2000

46 x 42 inches (1.2 x 1.1 m)
Old linen; hand dyed, appliquéd, top stitched

Photos by Bruno Jarret

▲ **La Lucarne** | 2001

62 x 45 inches (1.6 x 1.1 m)
Old linen, hemp; hand dyed, appliquéd, pleated, top stitched
Photos by Bruno Jarret

ANNE WORINGER

▲ **Genese** | 1988

62 x 62 inches (1.6 x 1.6 m)
Cotton; machine pieced, hand quilted

Photo by artist

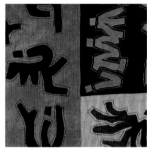

◀ **Les Mains Négatives** | 2000

50 x 56 inches (1.3 x 1.4 m)
Old linen, hemp; hand dyed, pieced,
appliquéd, top stitched

Photos by Bruno Jarret

Les Versets Hermétiques | 1999 ▶

49 x 72 inches (1.3 x 1.8 m)
Old linen, hemp; hand dyed, appliquéd,
top stitched, machine embroidered

Photos by Bruno Jarret

ANNE **WORINGER**

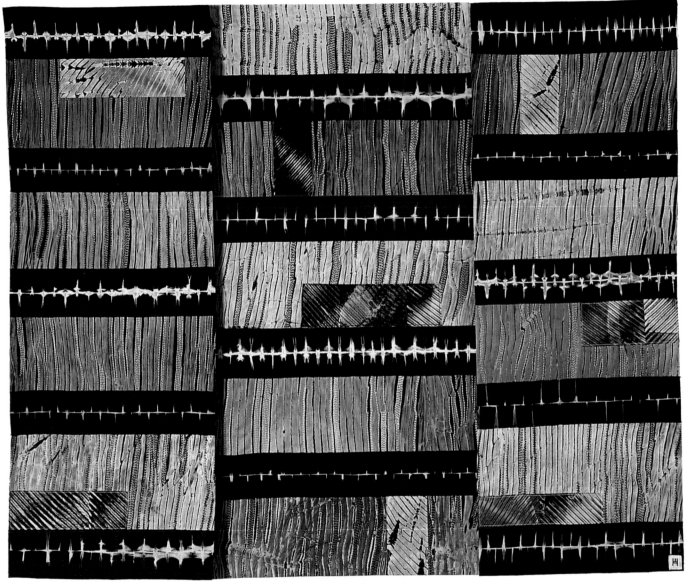

▲ Les Fascines | 2004

50 x 60 inches (1.3 x 1.5 m)
Black cotton; itagime shibori discharged,
hand embroidered

Photos by Bruno Jarret

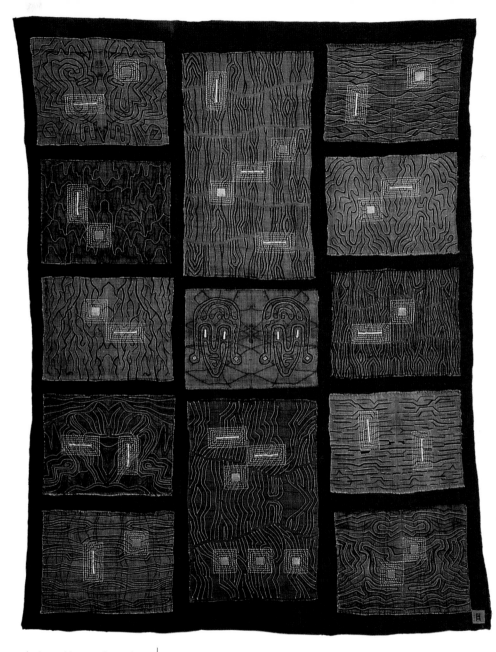

" My technique of fragmentation was dictated at first by the traditional log cabin, strip piecing, and the crazy quilt, which features the play of chance and spontaneity. At the same time, influenced by African-American quilts, I've tried to give flexibility to my constructions, to make them lively, free from geometric stiffness, while using ethnic fabrics that give a baroque character to my work. "

▲ Les Hamadryades | 2002

64 x 50 inches (1.6 x 1.3 m)
Black Thai hemp; discharged, hand and machine embroidered
Photo by Bruno Jarret

▲ Hurlevent | 2006

58 x 58 inches (1.5 x 1.5 m)
Cotton voile; arashi shibori discharged,
machine pieced, hand embroidered and quilted
Photo by Bruno Jarret

▲ Les Algues Bleues | 2004

39 x 57 inches (99.1 x 144.8 cm)
Chinese indigo ramie; arashi shibori discharged,
hand embroidered and quilted

Photo by Bruno Jarret

" I discharge black and indigo fabrics, using an old
Japanese technique called shibori to obtain graphic lines
and unpredictable, mysterious marks that I contrast or
emphasize partly with embroidery. "

PLUG

Clare Plug

MOST ART QUILTERS USE FABRIC as their medium because they are drawn to its textural qualities. But in Clare Plug's work the repetition of very simple forms and an extremely limited color palette forces texture to become the focus. Using bleach to discharge over black—described by the New Zealander as the "national color"—Plug celebrates the rhythms, patterns, and emptiness of the Hawke's Bay coastline where she lives. By using gathered stones, torn strips, or the folds of the fabric itself as the discharge masks, Plug is able to create an illusion of depth and weight. A fascination with the regularity of patterns found along the shore, both natural and man-made, inspires her use of repetition within her work. Stones on the beach, ripples on the water, paths in formal gardens—all influence her. The seeming simplicity of her designs focuses the viewer's eye on the subtleties of the variations of the forms.

▲ Nocturne in G | 2002

39 x 74 inches (99.1 x 188 cm)
Cotton, cotton batting, commercial cotton backing; discharge dyed, machine reverse appliquéd and quilted

Photos by Clive Ralph

▲ **To R.H. 2** | 2004

55½ x 70 inches (1.4 x 1.8 m)
Cotton, cotton batting, commercial cotton backing; discharge dyed, machine pieced and quilted

Photos by Clive Ralph

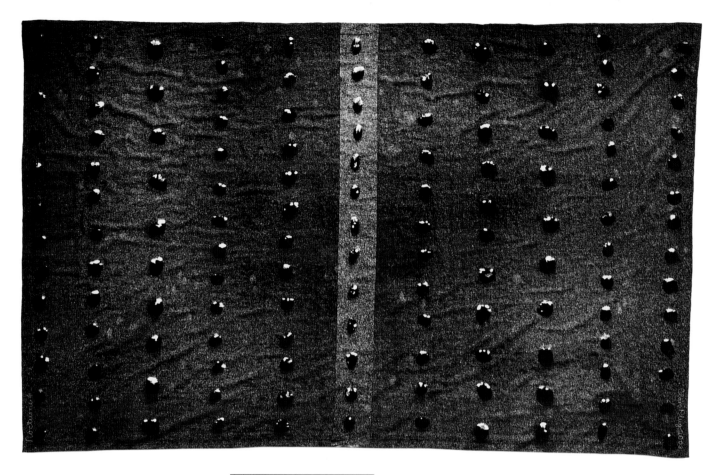

▲ **Nocturne 2** │ 2003

    29 x 44½ inches (73.7 x 113 cm)
Cotton, cotton batting, commercial cotton backing; discharge dyed,
machine pieced and quilted

    Photos by Clive Ralph

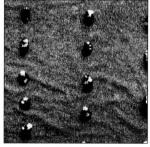

" In creating my artworks, I am drawing from the
long-established design traditions and conventions
of quilt making: processes of abstraction, graphic
effects, creation of optical illusions, compositional
devices used in the organizing of design elements,
an emphasis on real and visual texture, and the
use of repetition to generate visual rhythms. "

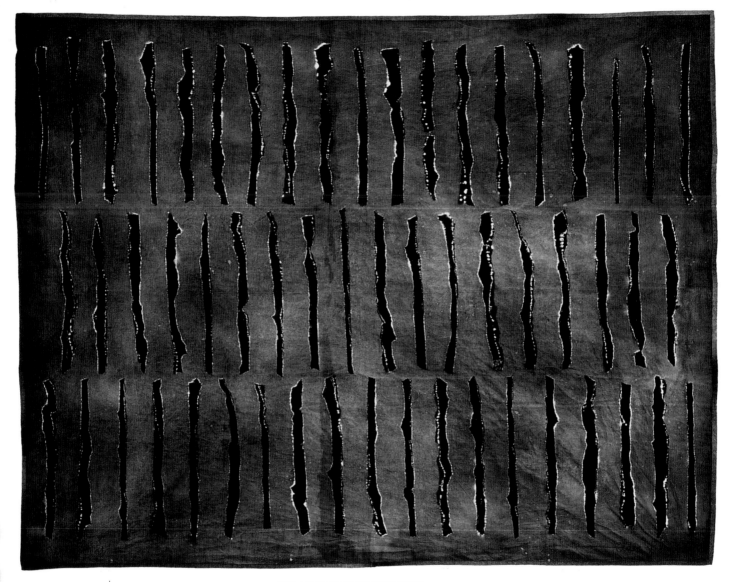

▲ **Night Beat** | 2000

46 x 57 inches (1.2 x 1.5 m)
Cotton, cotton batting, commercial cotton backing, whole cloth; discharge dyed, machine quilted

Photos by Clive Ralph

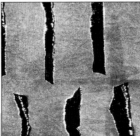

▲ Slip | 2002

43 x 57 inches (1.1 x 1.5 m)
Cotton, cotton batting, commercial cotton backing;
discharge dyed, machine pieced and quilted

Photos by Clive Ralph

" I continue to use this medium because I can do things here that I could not achieve in any other artistic medium. I feel a tremendous empathy for its numerous and unique properties. Textiles for me are about texture. I can convey moods, emotions, and ideas with great subtlety, often subliminally. "

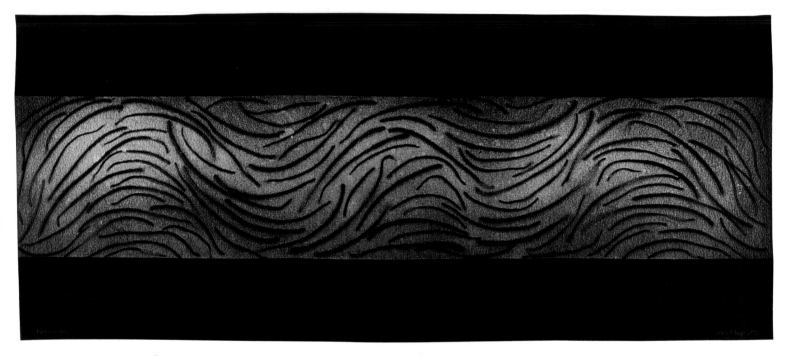

▲ **Promenade** | 2002

39½ x 94 inches (1 x 2.4 m)
Cotton, cotton batting, commercial cotton backing; discharge dyed, machine pieced and quilted
Photos by Clive Ralph

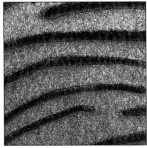

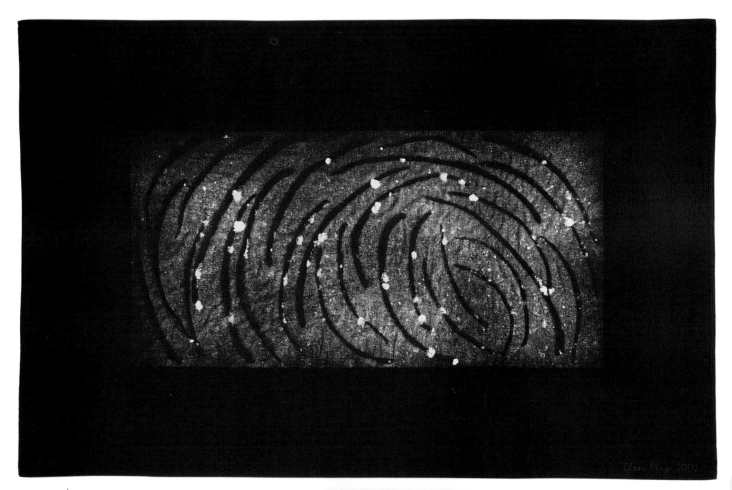

▲ Pool | 2002

38 x 59 inches (96.5 x 149.9 cm)
Cotton, cotton batting, commercial cotton backing;
discharge dyed, machine pieced and quilted

Photos by Clive Ralph

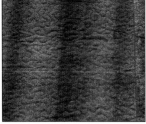

▲ **Suburban Rhythm** | 2007

68½ x 45½ inches (1.7 x 1.2 m)
Cotton, cotton batting, commercial cotton backing;
discharge dyed, machine appliquéd and quilted

Photos by Clive Ralph

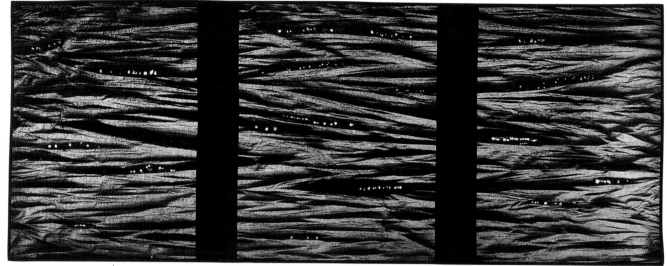

▲ **Scapa Flow 2** │ 2002

37 x 94 inches (94 x 238.8 cm)
Cotton, cotton batting, commercial cotton backing; discharge
dyed, machine pieced, appliquéd and quilted

Photo by Clive Ralph

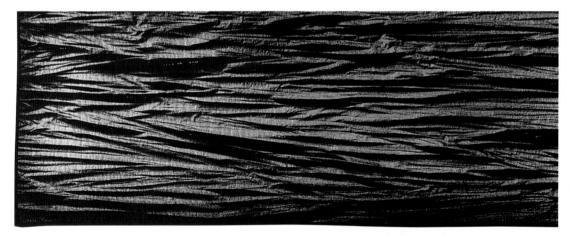

▲ **Scapa Flow** │ 2002

40½ x 96 inches (1 x 2.4 m)
Cotton, cotton batting, commercial cotton backing,
whole cloth; discharge dyed, machine quilted

Photos by Clive Ralph

Elizabeth Brimelow

ROWS OF CROPS, PLOWED FURROWS, and lines of apple trees all produce their own visual rhythm. This patterning of cultivated land is what inspires Elizabeth Brimelow. While much of her work has used more traditional appliqué, the British artist's most recent pieces use confetti-like strips trapped in tulle to depict cropland rows. *Fakenham Fen*, chosen for Quilt National 2005, takes this concept a step further and traps the confetti strips between two sheets of tulle, making the pattern occur in the middle of the quilt, an inversion of the usual process of quilt making which puts patterning on the outsides and hides the middle. Brimelow's decision to split the composition vertically into an uneven diptych creates a visual tension against the rhythmic diagonal repetition of the crop rows. Inspired by the farmlands she sees during walks in the area surrounding her home in East Anglia, Brimelow's work speaks of her deep and nurturing ties to the land. She says, "Landscape is where I live, what I look at, what I draw, and what I stitch."

▲ Low Meadow │ 2004

69 x 52½ inches (1.8 x 1.3 m)

Silk; hand and machine stitched, direct appliquéd, screen-printed, hand knotted

Photos by Michael Wicks

▲ Fen | 2003

57 x 57 inches (1.5 x 1.5 m)
Silk whole-cloth quilt, commercial, antique, and hand-dyed fabrics;
hand and machine stitched, hand quilted and knotted

Photo by artist

▲ Fakenham Fen | 2004

77 x 65 inches (2 x 1.7 m)
Silk, cotton, blends, paper nylon,
sequins, beads; hand appliquéd and
knotted, machine and hand stitched
Photo by Michael Wicks

" Landscape is physically determined by
geology that dictates the configuration
of its surface. Nature and history have
helped shape fields, wood, paths, and
open spaces. Land also is affected
by people. Plowing and harvesting,
building, excavating, and planting are
examples of interventions that have
left their own associated landmarks. "

Winter Wheat | 2005 ▶

46½ x 45½ inches (1 x 1.2 m)
Silk; hand and machine stitched,
direct appliquéd, hand knotted
Photo by Michael Wicks

▲ **Elsworth** | 1996

70 x 70 inches (1.8 x 1.8 m)
Wool, silk double-sided quilt; dyed, discharged, screen-printed,
direct and reverse appliquéd, hand and machine stitched, hand
quilted and tied

Photos by artist

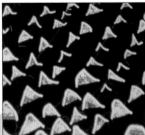

▲ **Appeltrebankes** | 1999

84 x 84 inches (2.1 x 2.1 m)
Silk double-sided quilt; hand and machine
stitched, direct and reverse appliquéd, slashed

Photos by Peter Jenion

▲ **Maravu** | 2000

60 x 60 inches (1.5 x 1.5 m)
Silk double-sided quilt; hand and machine stitched,
direct and reverse appliquéd, hand tied

Photo by Peter Jenion

▲ Reverse side

" Drawing is my response to my subject, and I aim to produce some of the qualities in cloth that I have created on paper. The words 'disclose,' 'lay open,' 'reveal,' 'discover,' and 'uncover' have been important in influencing my textile techniques. "

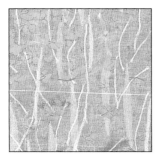

▲ Gaudy Ground | 2005

59 x 50 inches (1.5 x 1.3 m)
Silk; hand and machine stitched, direct
appliquéd, screen-printed, hand knotted

Photos by Michael Wicks

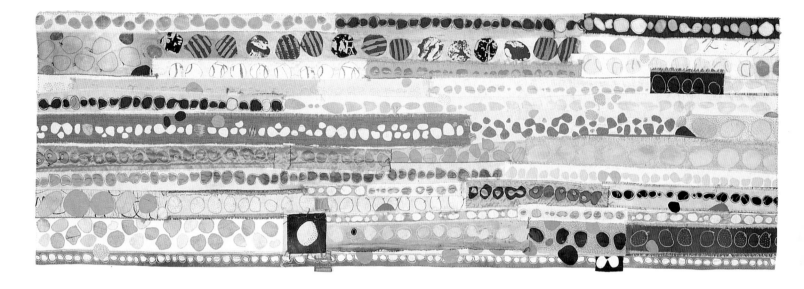

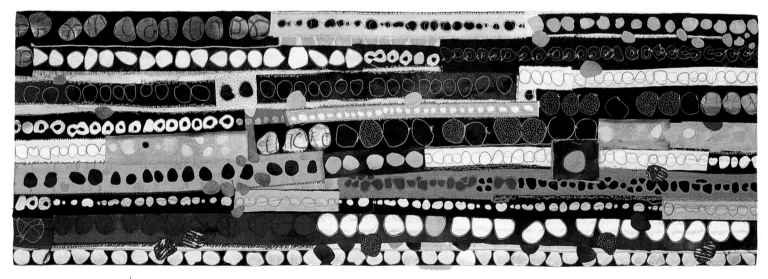

▲ **Shingle 1 and 2** | 2007

Each panel, 21½ x 62 inches (54.6 x 157.5 cm)
Silk, cotton, wool, linen, fabric by Heide Stoll-Weber; hand and machine stitched, direct
and reverse appliquéd, fused, screen-printed, hand dyed and knotted
Photo by Michael Wicks

▲ Peach, Pear, Plum | 2006

60 x 55 inches (1.5 x 1.4 cm)
Silk whole-cloth double-sided quilt; hand and machine stitched,
direct and reverse appliquéd, fused, slashed, knotted

Photos by Brian Blauser

"Fiber has been grown, spun, woven, dyed, and stitched for thousands of years. Stitching can represent a drawn line, alter a surface, or flood color into a piece. Through my hands, I have a story to tell, and this connects me to other times, cultures, and places."

▲ Reverse side

About the Curator

MARTHA SIELMAN HAS WORKED as an art quilter, art-quilt teacher, curator, author, and administrator. Her work has been exhibited in the United States and Central America and is in several corporate and private collections. Her pieces have been featured in *American Craft* and on the cover of *Art Calendar*.

As an art-quilt educator, Sielman has taught in preschool, elementary, and middle schools as a Master Teaching Artist with support from the Connecticut Commission on the Arts (now known as the Connecticut Commission on Culture and Tourism). Sielman has appeared on the HGTV show *Simply Quilts*, as well as on the local TV show *Artists and Authors*. Her articles about art quilts have been published in *The Crafts Report* and in the *SAQA Journal*.

In 2002, she founded Fiber Revolution, a group of art quilters who work together to educate the public about art quilts and to find exhibition opportunities. Over the next two years the group grew to 35 members living in Massachusetts, Connecticut, New York, Delaware, and Pennsylvania.

In May 2004, Sielman became Executive Director of Studio Art Quilt Associates (SAQA), a nonprofit organization dedicated to advancing art quilting as a fine-art medium. As SAQA's Executive Director, Sielman has witnessed the explosive growth of art quilting, as well as growing interest in art quilts as a legitimate and collectible fine-art medium.

Sielman lives in Storrs, Connecticut, with her husband, their five children, and two cats.

▲ **Jellies of Monterey** | 2003
42 x 31 x 3 inches (106.7 x 78.7 x 7.6 cm)
Hand-dyed cotton, silk, polyester cording, wire, paint; machine quilted, appliquéd
Photo by Richard Bergen

Acknowledgments

Without the 41 talented artists who contributed to the book, this volume would never have seen the light of day. We value their generosity.

Amanda Carestio, Dawn Dillingham, Delores Gosnell, Julie Hale, Rosemary Kast, and Kathleen McCafferty, along with editorial intern Laura Cook, provided tireless, top-notch editorial assistance. Their attention to detail kept the book on track. We're also grateful for the team of art production assistants Jeff Hamilton, Avery Johnson, Travis Medford, and Bradley Norris, who gave their unwavering support at every step of the process.

Finally, thank you to the photographers whose portraits of the quilt artists appear in this book:
B.J. Adams, photo by Gladstone, Australia
Eszter Bornemisza, photo by Aron Levendel
Elizabeth Brimelow, photo by Brian Ollier
Pauline Burbidge, photo by Keith Tidball
Cher Cartwright, photo by Megan Cartwright
Jette Clover, photo by Pol Leemans
Jane Burch Cochran, photo by Randy Cochran
Linda Colsh, photo by Fotostudio Leemans
Judith Content, photo by Reed Content
Chiaki Dosho, photo by A. Daisuke
Noriko Endo, photo by Nagamitsu Endo
Nancy N. Erickson, photo by Ron Erickson

Jeanette Gilks, photo by Stephanie Stein
Jenny Hearn, photo by Dion Cuyler
Steen Hougs, photo by Inge Mardal
Inge Hueber, photo by Roland Hueber
Wendy Huhn, photo by John Bauquess
Michael James, photo by Stenbakken Photography
John W. Lefelhocz, photo by T. Creamer
M. Joan Lintault, photo by Felicia Flanagan
Terrie Hancock Mangat, photo by Singeli Agnew
Carolyn L. Mazloomi, photo by Robert Giesler
Velda E. Newman, photo by Steve Buckley
Katie Pasquini Masopust, photo by Carolyn Wright
Yvonne Porcella, photo by Sharon Risedorph
Jane Sassaman, photo by Gregory Gantner
Deidre Scherer, photo by Jeff Baird
Joan Schulze, photo by Sharon Risedorph
Anne Woringer, photo by Philippe Lambert
Charlotte Yde, photo by Steen Yde
Ita Ziv, photo by Ela Ziv

The photos of Pamela Allen, Hollis Chatelain, Kyoung Ae Cho, Michael A. Cummings, Caryl Bryer Fallert, Inge Mardal, Therese May, Miriam Nathan-Roberts, Clare Plug, and Susan Shie are self-portraits.

Contributing Artists